From Intent to Action

From Intent to Action

The Management of Strategic Issues
in the Public Sector

Editors
Richard Boyle
Tony McNamara

Proceedings of the Institute of Public
Administration National Conference 1996

First published in 1996
by the
Institute of Public Administration
57-61 Lansdowne Road
Dublin 4
Ireland

British Library Cataloguing in Publication Data
A catalogue record for this book is available from the British Library

ISBN 1 872002 58 7

Cover designed by Butler Claffey Design, Dun Laoghaire
Typeset by the Institute of Public Administration
Printed by Smurfit Print, Dublin.

Contents

Contributors

John Bryson is professor of planning and public affairs at the Hubert H. Humphrey Institute of Public Affairs at the University of Minnesota.

Donal de Buitleir is General Manager, Office of the Group Chief Executive, AIB Group.

John Fitzgerald is the Dublin City Manager.

Frank Litton is a senior lecturer in politics and organisational theory in the Institute of Public Administration.

Frank Ryan is a senior training specialist in the Local Government Unit of the Institute of Public Administration.

Colin Talbot is professor of public management in the Business School of the University of Glamorgan.

Paddy Teahon is Secretary of the Department of the Taoiseach.

Brendan Tuohy is Assistant Secretary in the Department of Transport, Energy and Communications.

Foreword

The 1996 National Conference of the Institute of Public Administration, held at Jurys Hotel, Dublin, on 21 June 1996, addressed the theme *From Intent to Action: The Management of Strategic Issues in the Public Sector.*

The conference was held a short time after the publication of *Delivering Better Government*, the report to government from the Coordinating Group of Secretaries on the Strategic Management Initiative. The clear purpose of the conference was to move the discussion of strategic management in the public service to a consideration of the implementation stage. Significant energy has been invested in the devising of strategies, as evidenced in the report from the Coordinating Group of Secretaries. The challenge is now one of implementation. It is time to move from intent to action.

The issues which implementation pose for public servants differ significantly from those presented by the planning process. This became abundantly clear in the course of the presentations at the conference. Implementation must be planned (difficulties, obstacles and opposition must be anticipated); resources must be assigned (particularly, personnel who can champion it); due account must be taken of previous planning processes and their legacies.

The papers in this collection, we hope, will be a useful contribution both to deliberation and action on strategic management throughout the Irish public service.

The Institute of Public Administration is grateful to the contributors who made the conference a success, to the Minister of State with responsibility for the Strategic Management Initiative, Avril Doyle TD, who opened the conference, and to Professor Brian Farrell who chaired the proceedings.

Opening Address

Minister for State Mrs. Avril Doyle, TD

There is a well known piece of wisdom in the field of public relations and management training where the speaker is advised, if he is to get his message across during a presentation, to follow a well-proven sequence: first tell them what you are going to tell them; then tell them; then tell them what you have told them.

Strategic management seems to present us with much the same phenomenon. First, we talk about what we ought to be doing. Then we talk about what we are doing. Then we talk about what we should have done.

This kind of 'strategic management' is familiar to all of us. Of course, we like to think that other organisations are afflicted by this particular virus, but not our own!

It is probably through this kind of corporate self-deception that the virus manages to spread so easily.

Seminars and conferences give us a chance to explore what strategic management is really about. And I very much appreciate the opportunity to open these proceedings. By hearing how others have fared, and the mistakes they have made, we can begin to appreciate that strategic management is quite a complex concept. It is a great deal more than just an improved approach to planning. Neither can it be described as just a more efficient or more coordinated approach to management. Rather, it is primarily a means of systematically holding up to ongoing scrutiny the objectives which guide the organisation and the procedures which underpin it. And this is a tall order, given that we are required constantly to question our own worth and subject our successes and especially our failures to critical scrutiny. Whatever about our successes, none of us like to rake over the 'why' and 'wherefore' of our failures. However, if strategic management is to succeed, we must do just that.

The mistaken application of strategic management can result in a detailed planning exercise which somehow induces management to assume that all key problems facing the organisation have now been resolved. This kind of approach kills the hunger for problem solving on which good management thrives. It gets everything in reverse. We need to remember that planning exists merely to chart the way ahead and, invariably, to initiate a process of change; in itself it resolves nothing.

This reminds me of a fabled bird which has the uncommon facility of flying backwards. It does not care where it is going, it just wants to see where it has been.

Too much introspection can all too easily make us enjoy flying backwards and marvelling at our past achievements. If strategic management is to bear results, however, it must exist in a culture which *looks forward* to change and the many challenges which change implies.

Delivering Better Government

This brings me to the challenge of change initiated in May (1996) by the announcement of the government's programme of change for the civil service, *Delivering Better Government*. Rather than tackling the need for change on a piecemeal basis, the government decided to review the system as a whole and formulate a framework in which a systematic approach could be taken to innovation in general.

The process itself began with the Strategic Management Initiative – or SMI – in 1994, whereby each department identified its main objectives and the strategy needed to support them. Last year the IPA conference reviewed the SMI process and its progress but, as recognised then, the SMI threw up a range of issues and problems common to more than one department. Accordingly, the government mandated the Coordinating Group of Secretaries, set up to oversee and coordinate the SMI, to come forward with proposals to address these problems in a holistic and strategic way. Having examined the group's proposals in some depth, the government endorsed them.

From Planning to Action

We are now at a stage where we are addressing the very theme of this seminar, namely, how to get from the planning board to implementation. Both the government and the Coordinating Group were alive to this issue from the beginning. For this reason, *Delivering Better Government* includes a number of provisions which are designed to ensure that the processes initiated within the framework it lays down maintain their momentum and that the various elements cohere in a mutually supportive way.

But how can we be confident that *Delivering Better Government* will succeed where previous initiatives bore only limited results? In my opinion, there are several factors at work which I feel will ensure that the change programme for the civil service will carry itself successfully through to implementation.

Firstly, it has support across the political spectrum. This will be essential if it is to receive the ongoing commitment and attention needed to draw it all the way from aspiration to implementation.

3

It will need that long-term support because it will take many years, and quite a few governments, to see to its ongoing implementation.

Secondly, it is firmly placed within, and is supported by, the SMI process already underway in departments. There is, therefore, an evolving mechanism in place that is capable of supporting and reinforcing corporate change. Indeed, a key feature of advancing the programme is its interaction with the SMI process and the mutual dependence between them. If *Delivering Better Government* can be said to be predicated on a single idea, it is the principle that even in well-run organisations, further improvements are possible provided the culture and the structures are amenable to change. At the end of the day, Strategic Management is all about change – well-informed, well-planned and well-managed change.

Thirdly, every department will publish, by end 1996, a Strategy Statement setting out its mission, objectives and guiding strategies for the next several years. These statements involve each department revisiting and updating its earlier SMI statement and linking its strategies with those of *Delivering Better Government.*

This action alone will generate an expectation, both within and outside the organisation, that change is inevitable. It has long been known in the social and management sciences that expectation is a very powerful determinant of human behaviour, generating a momentum all of its own.

Fourthly, the expansion of the Coordinating Group to include senior figures from the public and private sectors, including the trade union movement, will ensure that the change process is kept consistently on target and that a strong sense of accountability prevails at all levels.

Finally, and perhaps most important of all, the entire programme will be underpinned by an active process of consultation with staff and customer interests. Consultation means listening and engaging in a meaningful dialogue; it is far easier to introduce change on the basis of consensus than through fiat and diktat. Indeed, the latter may only alienate the very people who can make change possible. Consultation also implies flexibility. *Delivering Better Government* is a framework to guide our thinking.

I would stress the need to approach the change programme, not as a microchip etched into silicon – to use a modern metaphor – but as an elaborate piece of computer software which may be modified and adjusted as required in the face of changing needs and circumstances.

Strategic management implies a consistent and systematic approach to change, which in turn implies teamwork and cooperation among all concerned.

It also implies accountability, openness and ongoing dialogue. I feel *Delivering Better Government* has all of these ingredients and that its future is assured.

Conference Theme

We must, however, learn from experiences elsewhere – we are by no means the first to embark on a major programme of change for the civil and public service. This conference is very welcome in this regard. The agenda is clearly action-oriented, putting the emphasis on converting plans into action and on the issues of managing strategically. One feature of the conference that I particularly welcome is the focus on strategic management in the public sector.

This is not to say that we cannot, and should not, learn from experiences in the private sector. But we must be alert to differences that exist between the two sectors, especially those differences which impact on the successful implementation and ongoing development of a strategic management approach.

Are the public and private sectors different? In so far as all organisations deal with objectives, targets, skills, resources, outputs and a range of similar issues, I believe they are not different. However, a key consideration is the culture and general climate in which business is conducted. For a number of very valid reasons, the public sector is far more likely to think of its senior staff as *administrators* rather than *managers,* to think in terms of established practices rather than innovation, to define activities in terms of programmes rather than targets and outcomes, and to measure results in terms of conformity rather than delivery. I have generalised a little here, but the distinctions I have made do highlight an important difference in culture and an approach which, up to recently, was not required to be very self-critical in appraising activities and to be proactive in changing course when circumstances so warranted.

Strategic management, therefore, calls for a somewhat greater effort initially from senior public servants than from their counterparts in the private sector.

The approach inherent in *Delivering Better Government* recognises this and is designed to raise the profile of change management and performance measurement, and to create a working environment where activities at all levels are guided by common, agreed and challenging goals. This means making better use of our resources and in particular the innovative skills and talents of public servants, notably those at the coal face and at middle management levels.

A conference such as this can do a great deal to aid and improve our understanding of how we should implement and advance strategic management in the public service. I congratulate the IPA on organising it at this time. As was the case with last year's conference, it is highly relevant to our needs at this juncture.

Implementing Strategies and Plans

John M. Bryson

Introduction

I propose to discuss how strategic planning can be converted to action. This is an important topic, and a difficult one to cover in a short paper, but I will do my best. Unfortunately, my best has resulted in a fairly long paper. Remember Thomas Jefferson's comment to a friend: 'If I had more time, I would have written a shorter letter.'

Most of my comments will focus on what governments might do, but I need to begin by asserting that when it comes to the most important public problems, improving government performance will not solve the problems. This is because the problems are bigger than any government.

When it comes to most important public problems, we live in a world where no one is fully in charge. Instead, many individuals, groups, and organisations are partially in charge, or have responsibility to act, or are affected by the consequences of action designed to address those problems. Consider some of the key issues mentioned in *Delivering Better Government : the Second Report to Government of the Coordinating Group of Secretaries* (1996): child care, drugs, employment, competitiveness, unemployment and social exclusion, financial services, and local development. It is clear that in each of these areas the government, civil service, and the broader public service are not in charge. They can help address these challenges, but they embrace only some of the people and organisations that must be involved if truly effective remedies to these problems are to be found. Put differently, *you cannot 'service' your way out of these challenges.* If public servants think they can, they are only kidding themselves – and doing the citizenry and democracy a disservice as well. They can be partners in addressing these problems and maybe at times a 'senior partner', but they cannot solve these problems by themselves.

The public sector therefore needs two broadly different sets of strategies if it is to meet the challenges the nation faces, and if the government's 'Vision for Ireland' (outlined in its policy agreement *A Government of Renewal* (1994)) is to be achieved. First, there is a need to provide higher quality government services, including policy advice. (This is true everywhere, not just in Ireland!) This I believe is the intent behind the title of the Coordinating Group of Secretaries' report *Delivering Better Government.*

Second, there needs to be a set of strategies for engaging the public broadly (that is, the public, private, and voluntary sectors, and the citizenry as a whole) in addressing the key challenges. Sometimes government might do this best simply by *getting out of the way.* At other times, government needs to act as a catalyst, providing crucial leadership, settings, or frameworks for action. At other times, government may need to provide specific *services and resources.* The point, however, is not only not to do what people can do for themselves, but to challenge and help them be *full citizens* – not just 'customers', or 'clients', or 'taxpayers', or 'voters' but citizens, who are as responsible for the public's work as the government is. In this view, *public work is more than the government's work*; and the people, the government, and other organisations in society need to join in doing the public's work. People can do public work on or off the job, for pay or not, with or without government involvement. The key point is that the public's work needs to get done, no matter who does it or how

(Boyte and Kari 1996). I think the spirit of this second set of strategies is captured in several ways in the government's 'Vision', but especially when it calls for 'extending the opportunities for democratic participation by citizens in all aspects of public life', and when it says, 'This programme for government will lead Ireland to become a more self-reliant, enterprising, and innovative society with a national self-confidence in our own ability'. Put differently, the purpose of the first set of strategies is to 'deliver better govern*ment*' while the purpose of the second set of strategies is to 'deliver better gover*nance*'.

Strategic planning is helpful in developing both sets of strategies. In this paper I will focus mainly on the first set of strategies for 'delivering better government'. First, I will discuss the typical desired outcomes and benefits of linking strategic planning to action. Second, I will emphasise the crucial role of *leadership* in making those linkages. Third, I will discuss two contrasting approaches to implementation planning, 'forward mapping' and 'backward mapping'. I will then discuss programmes and projects, budgets and strategic planning systems, followed by a number of guidelines for implementation. The paper closes with a short summary.

Desired Outcomes and Benefits of Linking Strategic Planning to Action

With that bit of context setting, let me move on to deal more directly with linking strategic planning to action by governments. Creating a strategic plan (if one has been created) is not enough; adopted strategies must be incorporated throughout the relevant system. Nor does strategy implementation have to wait until all the strategic planning is done. Whenever useful actions are identified, they should be taken. Continuous, effective leadership is mandatory throughout the formulation and implementation process. Developing effective programs, projects, action plans, budgets, and implementation processes and structures are also necessary if real value is to be created for the organisation (or community) and its stakeholders. Programs, projects, action plans, budgets, and implementation processes and structures are necessary in order to coordinate the activities of the numerous professionals, technicians, and frontline practitioners likely to be involved. Implementation should allow for adaptive learning as new information becomes available and circumstances change. Such learning will lead to more effective implementation – to better patterns (strategies) across purposes, policies, programmes, actions, decisions, or resource allocations – and to the cognitive and practical basis for emergent strategies and new rounds of strategising. Remember that realised strategies are a blend of what is intended with what emerges in practice (Mintzberg 1994).

The most important desired outcome which leaders, managers, and planners should aim for during implementation is real value-added through goal achievement and heightened stakeholder satisfaction. This will be accomplished through a series of more instrumental outcomes, including:

- Reasonably smooth and rapid introduction of the strategies throughout the relevant system and adoption of the changes by all relevant organisations, units, groups, and individuals in a timely fashion;

- Development of a clear understanding of what needs to be done, by whom, when, and why; statements of goals and objectives, a 'vision of success', and educational materials and operational guides all can help;

- Use of a 'debugging' process (or 'formative evaluation', Scriven 1967) to identify and fix difficulties that almost inevitably arise as a new solution is put in place;

- Use of 'summative evaluations' (Scriven 1967) – to find out if strategic goals actually have been achieved;

- Assurance that important features of adopted strategies and plans are maintained during implementation;

- Creation of redesigned organisational (or interorganisational, or community) *settings* that will ensure long-lasting changes; including the institutionalisation of implicit or explicit principles, norms, rules, decision-making procedures, and incentives; the stabilisation of altered patterns of behaviours and attitudes; and the continuation or creation of a coalition of implementers, advocates, and supportive interest groups who favour the changes;

- Creation of a new 'regime', if the redesign of the settings is significant. Regime construction is not easy and, therefore, will not happen unless the changes clearly are seen as 'worth it' by relevant implementers. A variety of new or redesigned settings that allow the use of a range of tools, techniques, and positive and negative sanctions or incentives may be necessary in order to shape behaviours and attitudes in desired directions;

- Establishment or anticipation of review points during which strategies may be maintained, succeeded, or terminated. Strategic management is a series of loops, not a straight line. Politics, problems and desired solutions often change (Kingdon 1995). There are no once-and-for-all solutions, only temporary victories. Leaders, managers and planners must be alert to the nature and sources of possible challenges to implemented strategies, and they should work for the maintenance of still-desirable strategies, replacement with better ones when possible or necessary, and termination of completely outmoded ones.

A number of important *benefits* flow from effective implementation:

- Successful goal achievement in which real issues are addressed smoothly and rapidly;

- Avoidance of the typical causes of failure, such as: resistance based on attitudes that are incompatible with desired changes;

11

personnel problems; poorly designed incentives; conflicts with pre-existing commitments of resources to other priorities; the absence of administrative support services; the absence of rules, resources, and settings for identifying and resolving implementation problems; and the emergence of new political, economic, or administrative priorities;

- Increased support for, and legitimacy of, the leaders and organisations that have successfully advocated and implemented the changes;

- Heightened self-esteem and self-confidence for the individuals involved in successful implementation. If a person has done a good job of addressing real needs, it is hard for him or her *not* to feel good about it. Professionals, in particular, derive a considerable portion of their work-related self-esteem and self-confidence from doing a good job. Effective implementation thus can produce extremely important 'psychic income' for those involved;

- Enhanced capacity for action in the future on the part of the organisations and people involved. They acquire an expanded repertoire of knowledge, experience, tools, and techniques and, therefore, are better positioned to undertake and adapt to future changes.

The Role of Leadership

Strategic planning is *not* a substitute for effective leadership. There is no substitute for effective leadership when it comes to planning and management. Instead, strategic planning is simply a set of concepts, procedures, and tools designed to help leaders, managers, and others think and act strategically on behalf of their organisations and their organisations' stakeholders. At its best, strategic planning helps leaders pursue virtuous ends in desirable ways so that the common good is advanced. At its worst, strategic planning drives out strategic thought and action, makes it more difficult for leaders to do their job, and keeps organisations from meeting their mandates and fulfilling their missions. Whether strategic planning helps or hurts depends on how leaders use it – or misuse it.

So what is leadership? I am particularly taken by Barbara Crosby's definition: 'Public leadership is the inspiration and mobilisation of others to undertake collective action in pursuit of the common good' (Bryson and Crosby 1992, p. 31). The definition makes it clear that *leadership* and *leaders* are *not* the same thing. Effective public leadership is a collective enterprise involving many people playing different roles at different times. Indeed, the same people will be leaders and followers at different times over the course of a strategic change effort.

The following interconnected leadership tasks must be performed well if strategic planning and implementation are to be effective:

- Understanding the context, including what the 'givens' are and what can be changed
- Understanding the people involved, including oneself
- Sponsoring the process by placing the necessary authority and power behind it
- Championing the process
- Facilitating the process
- Fostering collective leadership through the use of multi-member decision-making bodies and teams
- Using dialogue and discussion to create a meaningful process throughout the process
- Making and implementing decisions in the relevant areas
- Enforcing rules, settling disputes, and managing residual conflicts

- Putting it all together so that important issues are addressed and goals are achieved.

'Forward Mapping' and 'Backward Mapping'

Leaders, managers, and planners should consider two contrasting approaches to implementation planning, which Elmore (1982) calls 'forward mapping' and 'backward mapping'. A forward-mapping process begins at the top of the process, with as clear a statement as possible of the policy maker's intent, and proceeds through a sequence of increasingly more specific steps to define what is expected of implementers at each level. At the bottom of the process, one states, again with as much precision as possible, what a satisfactory outcome would be, measured in terms of the original statement of intent (Elmore 1982, p. 19).

There is a sound logic to forward mapping, and certainly, there are situations in which it makes sense. However, the major difficulty with forward mapping is 'its implicit and unquestioned assumption that *policy makers control the organisational, political, and technological processes that affect implementation*' (Elmore 1982, p. 20, original italics).

Clear lines of hierarchical authority and accountability are assumed. Forward mapping thus is problematic in many organisations – and certainly in multi-organisational networks or communities – where leaders and managers have influence only, not control, over the various implementation processes. In such situations much of what happens during implementation 'cannot be explained by the intentions and directions of policy makers' (p. 30) because it has very little to do with their intentions, and a great deal to do with the implementers' intentions and incentives.

An alternative approach is backward mapping, which begins not at the 'top' of an implementation process but at the very 'bottom', or 'street level', with a statement of the specific behaviour at the lowest level of the implementation process that generates the need for 'policy' (Elmore 1982, p. 21). Next, planners formulate an objective consisting of possible organisational actions at the lowest level that are likely to result in desired changes in behaviour, or effects, that would minimise the problem. Once the objective is formulated, planners go backward up the actual or possible structure of implementers or implementing agencies and ask two questions at each level. What is the ability of this unit to affect the behaviour that is the target of policy changes? What rules and resources does this unit need to create the desired effect?

Once these questions are answered, the final stage in the exercise is the formulation of a set of policies and strategies that direct or provide the necessary rules and resources to the units that are likely to have the greatest effects. Further, the exercise must involve explicit consideration of the settings likely to produce and protect desired changes. The source of the greatest effect, in other words, will be actors in settings – particularly those closest to the actual behaviour that create the issues that should be addressed – so those settings and the kind of behaviour leaders seek to influence within them must be given careful thought. Effective backward mapping can usually be seen in Total Quality Management (TQM) projects that begin with the customer and what he or she needs. It also can be seen in many open-ended citizen surveys and focus groups that try to reveal what the citizens want.

Backward mapping, like forward mapping, is concerned with what policy makers can do to produce desirable change. Backward mapping, however, does not assume that policy makers are the major influence on the behaviour of implementers or on the subjects of implementation. Nor does it assume that the appropriate measure of success is the policy makers' intentions; rather, it assumes that the appropriate measure is a reasonable estimate of what can be done in shared-power situations to influence change. The evaluation of policy makers', leaders', and managers' actions is thus less idealistic and more realistic. The logic of backward mapping – of 'turning implementation on its head' (Lipsky 1980) – should be kept in mind during earlier strategic issue identification and strategy development steps. If it is not, and only forward mapping is used, the policies and strategies that are developed and adopted are less likely to alter behaviour on the ground in directions that effectively address the real social problems or political needs the organisation faces.

It must be emphasised, however, that forward mapping and backward mapping are not antithetical. Indeed, planners should use both. Once they have worked backward, revealing the desired behaviour at the lowest level and the chains of influence-linkages that may produce that behaviour, the results of the analysis can be written up in a 'forward' fashion, as if they had followed that model. This allows them to recheck and elaborate the reasoning behind implementation plans, as they travel back down the influence chains. Both approaches have something to offer and should be considered by change advocates as they attempt to design, facilitate, and institutionalise lasting policy changes (Goggin et al 1990). Furthermore, the bottom-up approach may be helpful even when the policies to be implemented were developed in an exclusively forward, or otherwise impractical, way. Even in these situations, there often is enough flexibility available to implementers to justify a backward-mapping exercise designed to reveal practical ways to bring about change.

Programmes and Projects

Forward mapping and backward mapping likely to result in new or revised programmes and projects are a component of many strategic change efforts. Creation of programmes and projects is a way of 'chunking' (Peters and Waterman 1982) the changes by breaking them down into clusters – programmes – that consist of specific projects. Koteen (1989) refers to programme and project management as a form of 'bite-sized management', because the creation of programmes and projects can help clarify the design of a change initiative, provide a vehicle for obtaining the necessary review and approval, and provide an objective basis for evaluation of progress. Programmes and projects can also focus attention on strategic initiatives, facilitate detailed learning, build momentum behind the changes, provide for increased accountability, and allow for easier termination of what turn out to be undesirable initiatives. Of course, if drawing attention to the changes is unwise for any reason, a programme or project-management approach can still be used, but public relations strategy will need to be carefully thought through so as not to arouse the ire of powerful opponents.

Programme and project plans are a version of action plans. Koteen (1989, pp. 163-5) argues that programme and project plans should have the following components:

- Definition of purpose

- Calculation of desired inputs

- Definition of outputs to be produced

- Identification of target clientele

- Specification of objectively verifiable indicators

- Indicators of assumptions that are key to the success of the programme.

TQM and Business Process Reengineering (BPR) programmes are overarching and widespread approaches to enhancing governmental performance. Most of the US federal government has broad-ranging TQM efforts in place, as do many state and local governments. These efforts represent important means of enhancing performance – 'continuously improving' – in existing strategic directions (Cohen and Brand 1993). BPR represents a more radical kind of programme, or set of projects, in which strategies are often radically changed (Hammer and Champy 1993) in response to customer needs. BPR projects are becoming increasingly prevalent in US governments as they try to cope with increased demands and limited resources

The Special Role of Budgets

Budget allocations have crucial, if not overriding, significance for the implementation of strategies and plans. Budgets often represent the most important and consequential policy statements that governments or nonprofit organisations make. Not all strategies and plans have budgetary significance, but enough of them do for public and nonprofit leaders and managers to consider involving themselves deeply in the process of budget making. Doing so is likely to be a particularly effective way to affect the design, adoption, and execution of strategies and plans (Lynn 1987, pp. 191-3).

The difficulty of using budgets for planning purposes results partly from the political context within which budgeting takes place. The hustle, hassle, and uncertainty of politics means that budgeting typically tends to be short-term, incremental, reactive, and oriented toward accountability – rather than long-term, comprehensive, innovative, proactive, and oriented towards accomplishment of broad purposes, goals, or priorities. The politicised nature of budgeting is likely to be especially pronounced in the public sector, where adopted budgets record the outcomes of a broad-based political struggle among the many claimants on the public purse (Wildavsky 1984).

Another fundamental reason for the gap between budgeting and planning is that planning for control and planning for action are so *fundamentally different*, as Mintzberg (1994, pp. 67-81) argues, a 'great divide' exists between them. In Mintzberg's terminology, performance control consists of two hierarchies, budgets and objectives, while action planning consists of two other hierarchies, strategies and programs. The research evidence indicates that while it is hard to join either of the two pairs of hierarchies (budgets with objectives or strategies with programs), it is extremely difficult (and perhaps impossible) to join all four hierarchies together in a completely coherent, reasonable and workable way. Capital budgeting seems to be the only partial exception (in some cases) to this generalisation.

Performance control tends to be 'routine in nature, logically carried out on a regular basis, quantitative in approach and largely the concern of the accounting people, easily mapped onto the existing structure, and geared to motivation and control' (Mintzberg 1994, p.78). Further, this control is

> ... after-the-fact. In other words, objectives and budgets are not concerned with predetermining *specific* actions but with controlling overall performance, that is, with the cumulative consequences of many actions. Thus, they have little to do with the formulation of strategy *per se*. Rather, performance control constitutes an *indirect* way to influence the actions taken by an organisation (Mintzberg 1994, p. 78).

On the other hand, action planning is concerned with

> ... before-the-fact specification of behaviour: strategies are supposed to evoke programmes that are supposed to prescribe the execution of tangible actions ... In contrast with objectives and

budgets, strategies and programmes tend to be, if not nonquantitative, then at least less so, and more the purview of the line managers supported perhaps by the planners (pp. 78-9).

What can be done with the 'great divide', since both performance control and strategies and programmes are important? Several suggestions are possible:

Try to have strategy planning precede the budget cycle (Halachmi and Boydston 1991). Budgeting is more likely to serve overall organisational purposes if environmental assessments, strategic issue identification, and strategy formulation precede rather than follow it. The City of Milwaukee, Wisconsin, provides an excellent example of how this can be done for a large public organisation (City of Milwaukee 1995).

A key way to make this happen is to gain control of the 'master calendar' that guides formal organisational planning and budgeting efforts. As Lynn argues (1987, pp. 203-5),

> ... the master calender is the public executive's most important device for gaining ascendancy over the process of budget making in the organisation ... [because it] puts public executives in a position to spell out the assumptions, constraints, priorities, and issues they want each subordinate unit to consider in developing its programme, budget and policy proposals. In the process, they can define the roles of the various staff offices ... and indicate when and how they will make decisions and hear appeals.

Influencing the budget also depends on the personal strategising of public leaders and managers. Here again Lynn provides a useful insight, when he defines strategy as a 'set of value premises that constitute a source of direction or focus for the public executive's decisions and other actions' (1987, p. 139). Prior strategic planning efforts thus can provide many of the premises needed to try and influence budgeting in strategic directions (Halachmi and Boydston 1991; Bryson and Crosby 1992, pp. 81-117). And the short-term, incremental nature of budgeting actually can be a source of opportunity, rather than constraint, for the strategically-minded public leader and manager (Lynn, 1987, p. 203; Braybrooke and Lindbolm 1963). The system is a natural setting for organising a series of small wins informed by a strategic sense of direction.

Pick your budget fights carefully. Given the number of players that budgeting attracts, particularly in the public sector, it is not possible to win every battle. Attention therefore should be focused on those that are crucial to moving desired strategies forward. How the master calendar is organised and how attention is focused on budgetary allocations will strongly influence the way potential fights arise.

Attention is focused on budgetary allocations in three basic ways (Lynn 1987, pp. 208-9): Each has a different effect on the way issues are raised:

- *Each budget issue can be treated separately.* This means that issues typically would be framed and forwarded by subunits. The approach means that cross-issue or cross-unit comparisons are avoided, and it may be possible to hide particular choices from broad scrutiny. If resolution of the individual issues leads to exceeding the total resources available, across-the-board cuts or selective comparisons on the margin are possible.

- *Particular issues can be selected in advance for detailed consideration during budget preparations.* The strategic planning process would be a likely candidate for careful review. The typically incremental nature of budgeting might be influenced by the general sense of direction that emerges from addressing these issues.

- *Budgetary issues can be examined in the light of a comprehensive analytical framework or strategy.* Here the attempt is to influence

21

budgetary allocations based on a larger strategic vision. This approach is most likely to work when the strategic planning process can be driven by the idealised scenario approach and there is strong leadership in place to follow through with the vision of success that is likely to result.

* *Consider implementing 'entrepreneurial budgeting' concepts to advance strategic purposes.* A number of governments in various countries around the world are experimenting with reforms likely to facilitate implementation of intended strategies, help new strategies emerge via innovation, enhance managerial autonomy along with accountability for results, and promote a new kind of entrepreneurial culture (Osborne and Gaebler 1992; Cothran 1993).

Governments using these approaches begin by establishing broad strategic goals, and then setting overall expenditure limits, along with broad allocations for specific functions, such as health, public safety, or roads. Then, operating departments are given substantially increased discretion over the use of funds in order to achieve their portion of the strategic goals, 'subject to the usual constraints of legality and political prudence' (Cothran 1993, p. 446). This move significantly decentralises decisions. In a further shift from traditional practice, departments are allowed to keep a significant fraction of the funds left at the end of the fiscal year without having their budget cut. Cost savings and wise management thus can be rewarded and the 'use it or lose it' phenomenon of foolish buying sprees at the end of the fiscal year is avoided. In a further move to enhance cost savings and wise management, some governments allow individual employees to take a fraction of any savings they produce as income. The final feature of entrepreneurial budgeting is an emphasis on accountability for results. In return for increased discretion, higher-level decision makers want greater evidence of program achievement and efficiency gains. As Cothran (1993, p. 450) notes: 'Often an almost contractual agreement is negotiated between the central budget office and the operating departments, in which each department lists and ranks its objectives, specifies indicators for measuring the achievement of those objectives, and quantifies the indicators as much as possible'. If objectives are not achieved, serious questioning of managers by policy makers can ensue.

Entrepreneurial budgeting thus involves a blend of centralisation and decentralisation. Policy makers retain control over broad-scale goal setting and monitoring for results, while managerial discretion over how to achieve the goals is decentralised to operating managers. Authority is delegated without being relinquished; policy makers and managers are each therefore better able – empowered – to do their jobs more effectively (Carver 1990). In effect, as Cothran (1991, p.453) observes, 'entrepreneurial budgeting, and decentralised management in general, can lead to an expansion of power, rather than a redistribution of power'.

The changes that entrepreneurial budgeting are intended to induce are so profound that a shift in organisational culture is likely to result. Indeed, a major reason for moving to entrepreneurial budgeting is to create a culture of entrepreneurship, particularly in government (Osborne and Gaebler 1992). This change in culture itself needs to be thought about in a strategic fashion (Schein 1992; Hampden-Turner, 1990).

Make sure you have good analysts and wily and seasoned veterans of budgetary politics on your side (Lynn 1987, p.207). Budgeting is a complicated game and having a good team and good coaches can help the leader or manager interested in winning. There is really no substitute for having a savvy insider who can both prepare and critique budgets effectively. But while it is important to have good analysts and advisers, it is also important not to become their captive. The wise leader or manager will want to make sure that a sense of the organisation's desired strategy informs the analysts' and advisers' work.

Finally, to the extent that the same people are involved in both strategy formulation and implementation, the action-control gap is likely to be bridged. There are two approaches to doing this, one centralised, the other decentralised (Mintzberg 1994, pp.286-7). In the centralised approach, which is most closely associated with strong entrepreneurial or visionary leaders, the formulator does the implementing. By staying in close contact with the intimate details of implementation, the formulator can continuously evaluate and readjust strategy implementation. The decentralised approach, on the other hand, is more suitable for highly complex situations, in which 'strategic thinking cannot be concentrated at one centre' (ibid.). In this case, the implementers must become the formulators, as when 'street-level bureaucrats' determine a public service agency's strategy in practice (Lipsky 1980). At the extreme, this becomes what Mintzberg (1984, pp. 287-90) refers to as a 'grass-roots model of strategy formation'.

Strategic Planning Systems

Strategic planning systems are organisational mechanisms or arrangements for strategically managing the implementation of agreed-upon strategies. These systems, in other words, are themselves a kind of organisational (or interorganisational) strategy for implementing policies and plans. The systems also typically embody procedures and occasions for routinely reassessing those strategies. There appear to be five main types of systems, although *any strategic planning system in practice probably will be a hybrid of the five types.* The 'types' therefore refer to dominant tendencies. The types are:

- Layered or stacked units of management models
- Strategic issues management models

- Contract models
- Portfolio management models
- Goal or 'benchmark' models.

It is important to realise that each system embodies a set of arrangements that empowers particular actors, makes particular kinds of issues more likely to arise than others, and particular strategies likely to be pushed rather than others.

Before describing each approach I must express the ambivalence I have about attempts to institutionalise strategic planning management. While it often is important to create and maintain a strategic planning system, it also is important to guard against the tendency such systems have of driving out wise strategic thought and action – precisely those features that strategic planning (at its best) promotes. In practice the systems often become excessively formal, bureaucratic, driven by the calendar and not events, too numbers-oriented, captured by forecasts that are inappropriate, and conservative. The reader therefore is advised to keep in mind a key admonition: whenever any strategic planning system (or strategic planning process) threatens to drive out wise strategic thought and action, you should scrap the system (or process) and get back to promoting effective strategic thought and action.

Layered or stacked units of management models. The purpose of this approach is to effectively link inside and outside environments through development and implementation of an integrated set of strategies across levels and functions of an organisation. Figure 1 outlines a possible two-cycle layered or stacked strategic planning system. It represents the classic, private-sector, corporate style 'top down-bottom up' strategic planning process. In the first cycle, there is a 'bottom up' development of strategic plans within a framework of goals, objectives, and other guidance established at the top; followed by reviews and reconciliations at each succeeding level. In the second

Figure 1: Strategic Planning System for Layered or Stacked Units of Management

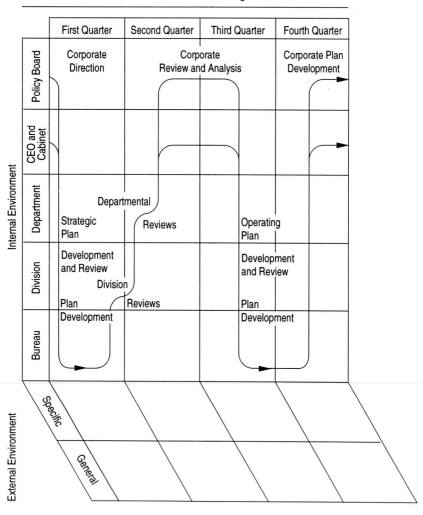

cycle, operating plans are developed to implement the strategic plans. In each cycle efforts are made to relate levels, functions, and inside and outside environments in effective ways. The process is repeated each year within the general framework established by the organisation's grand or umbrella strategies. Every three to five years these overarching strategies are reviewed and modified based on experience, changing conditions, and the emergence of new strategies that were not necessarily planned in advance.

Public organisations also have used variants of this approach to advantage. On the other hand, it is precisely this sort of system that is most prone to drive out strategic thought and action when it is underpinned by a belief that the future actually can be predicted accurately, a detachment from the messiness of operational reality, and excessive formality (Mintzberg 1994; Roberts 1993; Roberts and Wargo 1994). Such systems are very likely to be blind-sided by events which cannot be predicted, with the result that existing strategies and plans are thrown into a cocked hat. The systems therefore must be used with extreme caution, since they can take on a life of their own, promote incremental change when major change might be needed, and serve only the interests of the planners who staff them and the leaders and managers who wish to resist – not promote – major change.

Strategic issues management models. Strategic issues management systems are the most common form of institutionalised strategic planning and management systems in public organisations. These systems do not attempt to integrate strategies across levels and functions to the extent layered or stacked units of management approaches do. The reason is that the issues are likely to be on different time frames, involve different constituencies and politics, and not need to be considered in the light of all other issues.

A typical public sector strategic issues management system is the one used by Hennepin County, Minnesota (Eckhert, Haines, Delmont, and Pflaum 1993). In that system (see Figure 2) strategic guidance is issued at the top and units further down are asked to identify issues they think are strategic. Leaders and managers at the top then select which issues they wish to have addressed, perhaps reframing the issues before passing them on to units or task forces. Task forces then present strategic alternatives to leaders and managers, who select which ones to pursue. Strategies are then operationalised in the next phase. Each issue is managed relatively separately, although it is necessary to make sure that choices in one issue area do not cause trouble in other issue areas.

While many public organisations have several task forces in operation at any one time, fewer go the next step, to design and use a strategic issues management system. They do not establish an overall framework of organisational goals or policy objectives, seek out issues to address, or make sure their various issues-management activities add up to increased organisational effectiveness. Taking these steps can be quite beneficial, but organisational leaders and managers should keep in mind that the resulting centralisation of certain key decisions at the top is likely to draw the attention and resistance of those who do not want to see power concentrated in that way or who dislike the resulting decisions.

Contract models. The contact model is becoming an increasingly popular approach to institutionalising strategic planning and management (see Figure 3). It is the basic model for organising the National Health Service in the United Kingdom, where area boards assess health needs for their geographic area and then contract with health care units they directly control, independent health care trusts, physician group practices, and various nonprofit and voluntary organisations, for delivery of desired services. The contracting organisations may be inside or outside of the area (Pettigrew, Ferlie, and McKee 1992). The contract model also is employed for much of the planning and delivery of many publicly-financed social services in

Figure 2: Strategic Issues Management Model, Hennepin County

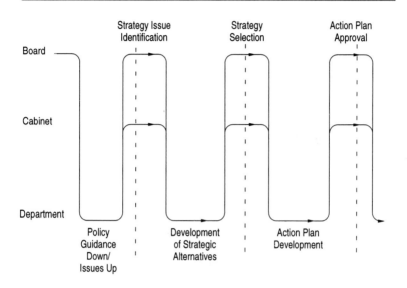

Figure 3: Purchaser-Provider Contract Model

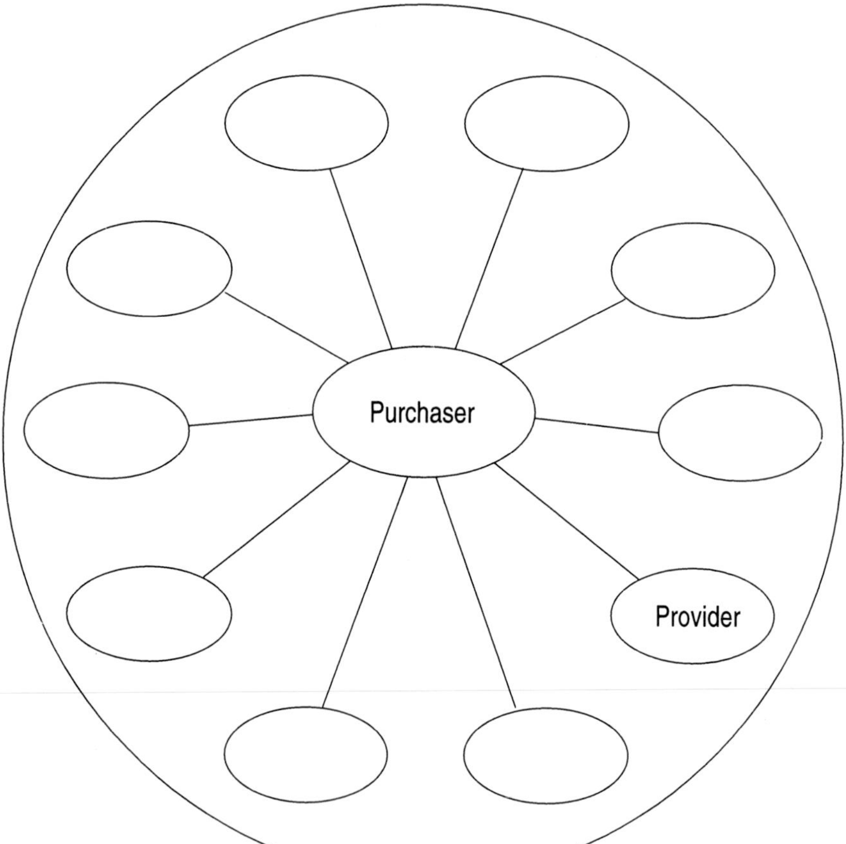

the US via either public or nonprofit service providers (Milward et al 1993). And the model is used to institutionalise strategic planning and management in school districts utilising site-based management.

In this model, a centre establishes strategic objectives for the jurisdiction or organisation as a whole, negotiates contracts with individual units of management, monitors performance, and ensures the integrity of the system. The contract between the centre and a unit outlines the unit's expected performance, defines its resources, lists other support the unit can expect from the centre, and describes a review and renegotiation sequence. Within the framework and legal strictures of the contract, general managers of individual units and their staffs are free to do whatever they think is necessary or desirable to ensure adequate performance. The approach allows both the centre and the individual units to focus on what is important for them; both are empowered to do their jobs better. In such a system, there would be a strategic plan for the centre and one for each of the units. Key system concerns will include the content and approach embodied in the centre's plan, the centre's difficulties in acquiring adequate information, and the difficulties the centre may have in exercising control in the face of a large number of contractors.

Portfolio management models. In this approach entities of various sorts (programmes, projects, products, services, or providers) are arrayed against dimensions that have some strategic importance. The dimensions usually consist of the attractiveness or desirability of the entity (from high to low) and the capability of the organisation or community to deliver what is needed.

Figure 4 shows one of the portfolios which was used to develop the three-year market strategy for the Royal Hospitals Trust in Belfast, Northern Ireland. The Royal is a self-governing trust that is part of the National Health Service system and must compete for the business it receives. The portfolio outlines the Royal's services in terms of

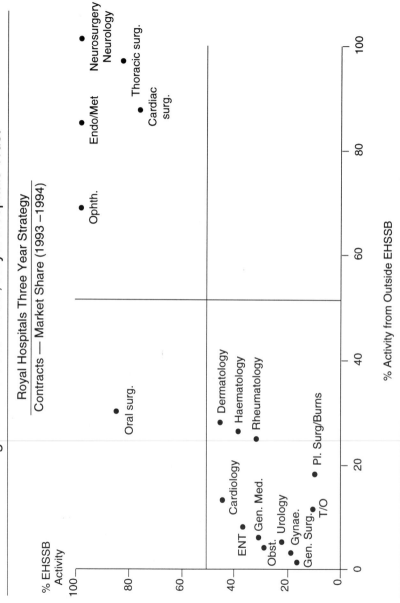

Figure 4: Portfolio Model, Royal Hospitals Trust

Royal Hospitals Three Year Strategy

Contracts — Market Share (1993 –1994)

% Activity from Outside EHSSB

% EHSSB Activity

desired market share for the three years beginning with 1993 in the Belfast (Eastern Health and Social Services Board) region. The Royal has or seeks a monopoly or near-monopoly in some services, such as neurosurgery and neurology, in the upper right-hand quadrant. It faces much more competition for the delivery of services in the lower left-hand corner. The Royal therefore has to have different strategies to manage those services than it does for those in which it has a stronger market position.

As the example from the Royal shows, portfolio methods are quite flexible, in that dimensions of interest may be arrayed against one another and entities mapped on to the resulting matrix. Portfolio methods also can be used at sub-organisational and supra-organisational levels as well to assess options against strategically important factors. Unfortunately, few public and nonprofit organisations and communities utilise formal portfolio models, even though many probably use informal portfolio methods. The problem, of course, with use of formal models is that they create comparisons that may be troubling for politically powerful actors.

Goal or benchmark models. In general, these approaches are also much 'looser' than the layered or stacked units of management models and are generally applied at the community or regional levels. They are designed to gain reasonable agreement on overarching goals or indicators (benchmarks) toward which relatively independent groups, units, or organisations might then direct their energies. Consensual agreement on goals and indicators thus provides a weak surrogate for the corporate control exercised in layered models. Nonetheless, when agreement can be reached and support for implementation can be generated, the models can work reasonably well. Besides, in the fragmented, shared-power environments in which most public problems occur, the approach may be the only viable one. For example, most community strategic plans in the US are implemented via goal or benchmark models. Typically, large numbers of leaders

33

and citizens are involved in the process of goal setting and strategy development. Then action plans outline what each organisation might do to help implement the strategies and achieve the goals on a voluntary basis.

The Oregon Benchmarks Program is a US state-level example (National Governors Association 1993; Oregon Progress Board 1995). In the Oregon program, a statewide and inclusive effort was undertaken to develop a set of goals and indicators that most Oregonians would support. The governor and the legislature expect state agencies to gear their plans and budget requests against the indicators. This feature is the 'tightest' part of the system. Cities, counties, communities, and others throughout the state are also encouraged to do their part. The success of the system depends on broad-based, bipartisan political support.

Again, remember that while there are five general types of strategic planning system, any actual system is likely to be a *hybrid* of all five types.

Process Guidelines

In previous sections, I have discussed some major topics important to implementing strategies and plans, including the importance of leadership, forward mapping and backward mapping, programmes and projects, budgets, and strategic planning systems. Now I would like to cover some general guidelines that should be kept in mind as adopted strategies or plans move to implementation. Throughout this section, keep in mind that successful implementation of strategies and plans will depend primarily on effective leadership and the design and use of various 'implementation structures' that coordinate and manage implementation activities, along with the continuation or creation of a coalition of committed implementers, advocates, and supportive interest groups (Goggin et al 1990; Bryson and Crosby 1992; Calista

1994). These structures are likely to consist of a variety of formal and informal mechanisms to promote implementation-created discussion, decision making, problem solving, and conflict management. New attitudes and patterns of behaviour must be established and adjusted to new circumstances, particularly through: the institutionalisation of shared expectations among key actors around a set of implicit or explicit principles, norms, rules and decision-making procedures; positive and negative sanctions and incentives; and the continuation or creation of a supportive coalition.

Also keep in mind that *implementation activities do not have to wait until all the strategic planning is done. Useful actions should be taken whenever they are identified.*

General Guidance

Consciously and deliberately plan and mange implementation in a strategic way. The implementers of the changes may be very different from the members of the advocacy coalition that adopted the changes. This is often the case when changes are 'imposed' on implementers by legislative or other decision-making bodies. Implementers thus may have little interest in making implementation flow smoothly and effectively. Further, even if implementers are interested in incorporating adopted changes within their respective systems, any number of things can go wrong. Implementation, therefore is hardly ever automatic. Consider journalist Robert Sherill's admonition: 'History is one damn thing after another'. Or poet William Blake's eloquent, 'Help! Help!' Implementation therefore must be explicitly considered prior to the implementation step, as a way of minimising later implementation difficulties, and it must be explicitly considered and planned for during the implementation step itself.

Implementers of the changes, particularly if they are different from the formulators, may need to engage in their own strategic planning process to figure out how best to respond to directives from others. This process should include efforts to understand and accommodate the history and inclinations of key formulators, implementing individuals and organisations (Neustadt and May 1986). Effective leadership will be necessary. Careful attention will also need to be given to organising programs and projects to effectively implement desired strategies. Budgets will also need to be given careful attention, if they are to help the organisation meet its mandates and fulfil its sense of mission.

Develop implementation strategy documents and action plans to guide implementation and focus attention on necessary decisions, actions and responsible parties. Strategies will vary by level. The four basic levels are: the organisation's or network's grand or umbrella strategy; strategy statements for constituent units; the programme, service, product, or business process strategies designed to coordinate relevant units and activities; and the functional strategies – such as finance, staffing, facilities, information technology or procurement strategies – also designed to coordinate units and activities necessary to implement desired changes. It may not have been possible to work out all of these statements in advance. If not, the implementation step is the time to finish the task in as much detail as is necessary to focus and channel action without also stifling useful learning.

Strategies may be long-term or short-term. Strategies provide a framework for tactics – the short-term, adaptive actions and reactions used to accomplish fairly limited objectives. Strategies also provide the 'continuing basis for ordering these adaptions toward more broadly conceived purposes' (Quinn 1980, p.9). Action plans are statements about how to implement strategies in the short term (Morrisey, Below, and Acomb 1987; Randolph and Posner 1988; Frame 1987). Typically action plans cover periods of a year or less. They outline specific tasks, the resources necessary to accommodate them, who is responsible, and the target completion date. Without action planning, intended strategies are likely to remain dreams, not reality. The intentions will be overwhelmed by already implemented and emergent strategies.

Try for changes that can be introduced easily and rapidly. Implementers may have little room for manoeuvre when it comes to the basic design of the proposed changes and the accompanying implementation process. Nonetheless, they should take advantage of whatever discretion they have to improve the ease and speed with which changes are put into practice, while still maintaining the basic character of the changes. Implementation will flow more smoothly and speedily if the changes:

- are conceptually clear;

- are based on a well-understood theory of cause-effect relations;

- fit with the values of all key implementers;

- can be demonstrated and made 'real' to the bulk of the implementers prior to implementation; in other words, people have a chance to see what they are supposed to do before they have to do it;

- are relatively simple to grasp in practice because the changes are not only conceptually clear, but also are operationally clear;

- are administratively simple, with minimal bureaucracy and red tape, minor reorganisations or impacts on resource allocation patterns, and minimal skill readjustments or retraining;

- allow a period of start-up time in which people can learn about the adopted changes and engage in any necessary retraining, debugging, and the development of new norms and operating routines;

- include adequate attention to payoffs and rewards necessary to gain wholehearted acceptance of implementers; in other words, there are clear incentives favouring implementation by relevant organisations and individuals.

Use a programme and project management approach wherever possible. 'Chunking' the changes by breaking them into clusters, or programmes, consisting of specific projects, is a typically important means of implementing strategic changes. Utilise standard programme and project management techniques to assure the 'chunks' actually add up to useful progress (Koteen 1989).

Build in enough people, time, attention, money, administrative and support services, and other resources to assure successful implementation. If possible, build in considerable redundancy in places important to implementation, so that if something goes wrong – which it no doubt will – there is adequate backup capacity. Almost any difficulty can be handled with enough resources – although these days budgets typically are exceedingly tight unless money can be freed from other uses. Think about why cars have seatbelts and spare tyres, jetliners have co-pilots, and bridges are built to handle many times more weight than they are expected to carry; it is to ensure enough built-in capacity to handle almost any unexpected contingency. Tight resources are an additional reason to pay attention to the earlier steps in the strategy change cycle. In order to garner sufficient resources, the issue must be important enough, adopted strategies must be likely to produce desirable results at reasonable cost, and the supportive volition should be strong and stable. If these elements are present, the chances of finding or developing the necessary resources for implementation are considerably enhanced. Nonetheless, there still may be resistance from those who must supply the resources, and considerable effort may be needed to overcome it. In almost every case, careful attention will need to be paid to budgeting cycles, processes, and strategy.

Implementation plans should include resources for:

- key personnel
- 'fixers' – people who know how things work and how to 'fix' things when they go wrong (Bardach 1977)
- additional necessary staff
- conversion costs
- orientation and training costs
- technical assistance
- inside and outside consultants
- adequate incentives to facilitate adoption of the changes by relevant organisations and individuals
- formative evaluations to facilitate implementation, and summative evaluations to determine whether or not the changes produced the desired results
- unforeseen contingencies.

Link new strategic initiatives with ongoing operations in effective ways. Establishing new units, programmes, projects, products, or services with their own organisational structures and funding streams is a typical strategy in the public sector. That way overt conflicts with ongoing operations can often be minimised. But in an era of resource constraints, new initiatives often must compete directly with, and be merged with, ongoing programmes, products, services, and operations of managers and their staffs. Unfortunately, the implications of a strategic plan for an organisation's ongoing operations may be very unclear, particularly in the public sector where policy-making bodies may impose rather vague mandates on operating agencies. Somehow new and yet often vague initiatives that have external support must be blended with ongoing priorities in such a way that internal support is generated on the part of those charged with maintaining the ongoing programmes, products, and services of the organisation. People staffing existing operations, however, are likely to feel overworked and undervalued already and therefore will want to know how the changes will help or hurt them. Typically they must be involved directly in the process of fitting desired strategic changes into the operational details of the organisation, both to garner useful information and support and to avoid sabotage.

One effective way to manage the process of blending new and old activities is to involve key decision makers, implementers, and perhaps representatives of external stakeholder groups in evaluating both sets of activities using a common set of criteria. At least some of these criteria are likely to have been developed earlier as part of the strategic planning process, and may include client and organisational impacts, stakeholder expectations, and resource use. Once new and old activities have been evaluated, it may be possible to figure out how to fit the new with the old, what part of the new can be ignored, and what part of the old can be dropped. Again, recall that realised strategy will be some combination of the intentions embodied in strategic plans, ongoing initiatives and the emergence of unexpected occurrences along the way.

Work quickly, to avoid unnecessary or undesirable competition with new priorities. The economy can always go bad and severely damage financial support for proposed changes, whether that support consists of tax revenues, subventions or grants from other organisations, or the markets for products and services that can be sold. The possibility that the economy can turn sour is yet another reason to build in extra resources for implementation. A poverty budget can turn out to be a death warrant. So, leaders, managers, and planners should not make cheapness a selling point. Instead, they should sell cost-effectiveness – that is, they must sell the idea that the programme delivers great benefits in relation to the costs expended and that, therefore, the costs, even if considerable, are worth it.

A change among policy makers, senior managers, or other key decision makers is also likely to bring a change in priorities (Schein 1992; Kingdon 1995). New positional leaders have their own conceptions of the issues that should be addressed and how this should be done. Further, the anticipation of having new key decision makers often paralyses any change effort. People want to see what will happen before risking their careers by pushing changes that may not be desired by new positional leaders. So, once again, leaders and managers must move quickly to implement new strategies and plans before actual or impending change in the economy or the political scene undermines the effort.

Focus on maintaining or developing a coalition of implementers, advocates, and interest groups intent on effective implementation of the changes and willing to protect them over the long haul. One of the clear lessons from the past two decades of implementation research is that successful implementation of programs in shared-power situations depends upon developing and maintaining such a coalition (Goggin et al 1990). Coalitions are organised around ideas, interests, and payoffs, so, leaders and managers must pay attention to 'coaligning' these elements in such a way that strong coalitions are created and maintained (Kotter and Lawrence 1974). Strong coalitions will result if those involved see that their interests are served by the new arrangements.

Assure that political and managerial arenas facilitate rather than impede implementation. It is important to maintain liaison with the decision makers in arenas where future decisions can affect the implementation effort. Leaders and managers in the implementation step must also pay attention to the development and use of supplemental policies, regulations, rules, guidelines, or other guidance necessary to implement the changes authoritatively adopted earlier. Operational details must be worked out, and many of them will need to pass through specific processes before they can have the force of law. Change advocates should seek expert advice on how these processes work and attend to the ways in which supplemental policies are developed. Otherwise, the promise of the strategic planning effort may be lost in practice.

Think carefully about how residual disputes will be resolved and underlying norms enforced. This, of course, may mean establishing special procedures and mechanisms for settling disputes that arise. It may also mean relying on the formal courts. It may mean relying on 'alternative dispute resolution methods' wherever possible, in order to keep conflicts out of the formal courts and open up the possibility of all-gain solutions that increase the legitimacy and acceptance of the policy, strategy, or plan and the outcomes of conflict management efforts (Fisher and Ury 1981; Susskind and Cruikshank 1987). The court of public opinion is also likely to be important in reinforcing the norms supporting the new changes.

Remember that major changes, and even many minor ones, entail changes in the organisation's culture. Changes in strategy almost inevitably will prompt changes in shared basic assumptions about organisational culture as a consequence of adapting to changes in the internal and external environments. Leaders, managers, and planners should attend to the need to facilitate necessary changes in cultural artifacts, espoused values, and underlying assumptions, while recognising that it is far easier to change the first two than it is to change the third. Indeed, heavy-handed attempts to change underlying assumptions are more likely to promote resistance and rejection than acceptance (Schein 1992; Hampden-Turner 1990).

Emphasise learning. The world does not stop for planning or once the planning is done. Situations change, and therefore those interested in change must constantly learn and adapt. Formative evaluations can facilitate necessary learning, but learning should also become a habit – part of the culture – if organisations are to remain vital and of use to their key stakeholders (Senge 1990; Schein 1992). To put it another way, strategies are hardly ever implemented as intended. Adaptive learning is necessary to tailor intended strategies to emergent situations so that appropriate modifications are made and desirable outcomes are produced (Mintzberg 1994).

Hang in there! Successful implementation in complex, multi-organisational, shared-power settings typically requires large amounts of time, attention, resources, and effort (Kingdon 1995), and implementers also may need considerable courage to fight the resisters of change. The rewards, however, can be great – namely, effective actions addressing important strategic issues that deeply affect the organisation and its stakeholders. The world is likely to be made better only through wise collective thought and action over the long haul.

Communication and Education

Invest in communication activities. This means attention to the design and use of communication networks and the messages and messengers that compose them (Goggin et al 1990). Particularly when large changes are involved, people must be given opportunities to develop shared meanings and appreciations that will further the implementation of change goals (Trist 1983; Sabatier 1991). These meanings will both guide and flow out of implementation activities. People must *hear* about the proposed changes, preferably hearing the same messages across multiple channels many times, to increase the chances that the messages will sink in. Further, people must be able to *talk* about the changes, in order to understand them, fit them into their own interpretive schemes, adapt them to their own circumstances, and explore implications for action and the consequences of those actions (Trist, 1983; Johnson and Johnson 1994). Educational programmes, information packets, and guidebooks can help establish a desirable frame of reference and common language for addressing implementation issues.

Work to reduce resistance based on divergent attitudes and lack of participation. Actions likely to reduce resistance on the part of implementers include providing those implementers with orientation sessions, training materials and sessions, problem-solving teams, one-to-one interactions, and technical assistance to support strategy implementation and overcome obstacles to it. Ceremonies and symbolic rewards to reinforce desired behaviours are also helpful.

Consider developing a guiding vision of success if one has not been developed already. Developing a vision of success is an exercise in 'rhetorical leadership' (Doig and Hardgrove 1987), and differing implementing units or structures may need their own.

Build in regular attention to appropriate indicators. This will assure attention to progress – or lack thereof – against the issues that prompted the strategic planning effort.

Personnel

As much as possible, fill leadership and staff positions with highly qualified people committed to the change effort. As noted, changes do not implement themselves; people make them happen. This is particularly true for major changes. When minor changes are required, systems and structures often can be substitutes for leadership (Kerr and Jermier 1978; Manz 1986). But when significant changes are involved, there are no substitutes for leadership of many kinds. People – intelligent, creative, skilled, experienced, committed people – are necessary to create the new order, culture, systems, and structures that will focus and channel efforts toward effective implementation.

Continue the team responsible for strategic planning or establish a new implementation team that has a significant overlap in membership. As indicated, successful implementation typically requires careful planning and management. In complex change situations, a team is likely to be necessary to help with this effort. If members involved in the effort to get new strategies adopted are included, it helps assure that important learning from earlier steps is not lost during implementation.

Assure access to, and liaison with, top policy makers and managers during implementation. This task is easy when the change advocates themselves are or become the top policy makers or managers. Even if they do not, they may find that administrators are interested in continued contact with them, either because the administrators have, or must have, the advocates' support.

Give special attention to the problem of easing out, working around, or avoiding people who are not likely to help the change effort for whatever reason. A standard practice in the public sector, of course, is to start a new agency rather than give implementation responsibilities to an existing agency whose mission, culture, personnel, and history are antagonistic to the intent of changes. For example, President Lyndon Johnson insisted on a new Office of Economic Opportunity rather than turn over implementation responsibilities for many of his Great Society programs to established agencies such as the Departments of Labour or Health, Education and Welfare. He remarked at one point: 'The best way to kill a new idea is to put it in an old line agency' (Anderson 1990, p. 180). Or, as management theorist Frederick Hertzberg often says: 'It is easier to give birth than to resurrect'. But even if a new organisation is started, leaders and managements may still be stuck with personnel who are detrimental to achievement of the policy goals. Special efforts will be necessary to deal with these people.

Direct versus Staged Implementation

There are two basic approaches to implementation, direct and staged. Direct implementation incorporates changes into all relevant sites essentially simultaneously, while staged implementation incorporates changes sequentially into sites.

Consider direct implementation when the situation is technically and politically simple, immediate action is necessary for system survival in a crisis, or the adopted solutions entail some 'lumpiness' that precludes staged implementation. When situations are simple, direct implementation can work if enough resources are built in to cover costs and provide sufficient incentives, and if resistance to change is low. Therefore, leaders and managers must try to reduce any resistance to change based on divergent attitudes and lack of earlier participation. A crisis can simplify a situation politically in that people become more willing to defer to top positional leaders and accept centralised decision making (Bryson 1981; Alterman 1995). This also makes direct implementation feasible. However, strategies adopted to address crises must still be technically workable, or at least practical enough so that difficulties can be worked out without weakening people's support for change. Unfortunately, few organisations have a crisis management system in place effective enough to respond adequately (Mintroff and Pearson 1993). Finally, lumpy solutions may demand direct implementation. For example, new buildings, information technology systems, and products or services must often be created all at once rather than piecemeal.

In difficult situations consider staged implementation. Staged implementation presumes that implementation will occur in 'waves', in which initial adopters will be followed by later adopters, and finally, even most of the laggards will adopt the changes. The result is the familiar S-shaped curve associated with the adoption of most innovations over time. Early on, there are few adopters, so the area under the curve is small. As time progresses, more and more adoptions occur, increasing the area under the curve geometrically, so that it begins to assume an 'S' shape. Later, fewer and fewer adoptions occur, partly because there are fewer people, units, or organisations left to adopt the changes, and partly because of deep-seated resistance on the part of the laggards. The curve levels off as the top of the 'S' is completed (Rogers 1982).

The exact nature of the staged process will depend on the difficulties faced. When facing technical difficulties, consider beginning with a pilot project designed to discover or to prove the cause-effect relations between particular solutions and particular effects. The more difficult the situation technically, the more necessary pilot projects are to figure out what techniques do and do not work. Once the technical difficulties are resolved, transfer of the implementation process to the remaining potential implementers can be pursued. For example, pilot tests of new US agricultural products and services occur regularly at agricultural experiment stations that involve universities, the US Department of Agriculture and business in cooperative partnerships.

When facing political difficulties, consider beginning staged implementation with demonstration projects to make it clear that solutions known to work in benign and controlled conditions can work in typical implementer settings. Once the generalisability of the changes is demonstrated, transfer to remaining implementers can be pursued. Demonstration projects are most likely to work when the existing or potential opposition is not well organised, because changes can be put in place before an effective opposition can materialise. When there is organised opposition to the proposed changes, demonstration projects may work as a way of convincing at least some opponents of the merits of the changes, thereby dividing the opposition. When there is a well organised and implacable opposition, direct and massive implementation efforts may be warranted – to expand the front and overwhelm opponents, rather than give them a limited number of smaller targets to oppose (Bryson and Delbecq 1979). However, while that may be the best approach, the chances of success in such situations still are not great (Bryson and Bromiley, 1993), given the likely strength of the opponents.

When facing both technical and political difficulties, consider beginning with a pilot project, followed by demonstration projects, followed by transfer to the rest of the implementers. In general, the more difficult the situation, the more important are: tactics aimed at education and learning; incentives for desired changes; and the development of a shared sense of commitment to successful implementation and long-term protection of the changes among all interested parties.

Finally, when the implementation process is staged, give special attention to those who will implement changes in the early stages. In the early stages, when the practical nature of the changes still need to be worked out, it is important to attract people with enough experience, skills, and desire to make the changes work. People who are likely to do so will have: first-hand experience with the issue and the need for an adequate response; above-average ability; and experience with prior major change efforts. Further, later adopters will be watching to see whether or not they wish to embrace the changes or resist them. Early implementers thus should be valued and persuasive role models. They are more likely to be effective salespersons for change if they do not mindlessly charge after every new whim and fad that comes over the horizon. Instead, they should be seen as courageous, wise, able and committed to addressing the issue in a reasonable way. Further, they should be able to describe their experience to effectively educate the next wave of adopters.

Summary

Desired changes are not completed with the adoption of strategies and plans. Without effective implementation, important issues will not be addressed adequately or at all. Implementation therefore should be viewed as a continuation of the strategy change effort toward its ultimate goal of addressing the issues that prompted change in the first place. Implementation must be consciously, deliberately, and strategically led, planned, managed, and budgeted – and does not have to wait until all the planning is done. Further, if major changes are involved, successful implementation typically involves creation of a new 'regime' to govern decisions and behaviour. Elements of the new regime will include: new or redesigned settings; the establishment of implicit or explicit principles, norms, rules and decision-making procedures; the development of supportive budgets and the use of substantive and symbolic incentives promoting the new arrangements; the institutionalisation of altered patterns of behaviour and attitudes; and continuation or creation of a supportive coalition of implementers, advocates, and interest groups. The new regime may incorporate a widely-shared vision of success.

Successful implementation introduces desired changes quickly and smoothly, and overcomes the typical causes of implementation failure. These strategies may involve either direct or staged implementation. Direct implementation works best when the time is right, the need is clear to a strong coalition of supporters and implementers, there is a clear connection between critical issues and adopted strategies, solution technology is clearly understood, adequate resources are available, and there is a clear vision to guide the changes. Staged implementation is advisable when policy makers, leaders, and managers are faced with technical or political difficulties. It often involves: pilot projects, to determine or to prove the cause-effect relations between particular solutions and desired effects;

demonstration projects, to show the generalisability of adopted solutions to typical implementer settings; diffusion of knowledge to later waves of adopters. Staged implementation involves organising a series of 'small wins'

Learning is a major theme underlying successful implementation efforts. It is not possible or desirable to plan everything in advance. People must be given the opportunity to learn and adapt adopted changes to actual situations on the ground. More effective implementation is likely to result, and the next round of strategising is likely to be better informed.

References

A Government of Renewal (1994), Dublin, Stationery Office

Alterman, R. (1995), 'Can Planning Help in Time of Crisis? Planners' Responses to Israel's Recent Wave of Mass Immigration', *Journal of American Planning Association*, 61(2), pp. 156-177

Anderson, J.E. (1990), *Public Policymaking*, Boston, Houghton Mifflin

Bardach, E. (1977), *The Implementation Game*, Cambridge, Mass, MIT Press

Boyte, H. and Kari, N. (1996), *Rebuilding America: The Democratic Promise of Public Work*, Philadelphia, PA, Temple University Press

Braybrooke, D., and Lindblom, C.E. (1963), *A Strategy of Decision: Policy Evaluation as a Social Process*, New York, Free Press

Bryson, J.M. (1995), *Strategic Planning for Public and Nonprofit Organisations*, Revised Edition, San Francisco, CA, Jossey-Bass

Bryson, J.M. (1981), 'A Perspective on Planning and Crises in the Public Sector', *Strategic Management Journal*, 2, pp. 181-196

Bryson, J.M. and Bromiley, P. (1993), 'Critical Factors Affecting the Planning and Implementation of Major Projects', *Strategic Management Journal*, 14, pp. 319-337

Bryson, J.M. and Crosby, B.C., (1992), *Leadership for the Common Good: Tackling Public Problems in a Shared Power World*, San Francisco, Jossey-Bass

Bryson, J.M. and Delbecq, A.L. (1979), 'A Contingent Approach to Strategy and Tactics in Project Planning', *Journal of the American Planning Association*, 45(2), pp. 167-179.

Calista, D.J. (1994), 'Policy Implementation', in S. Nagel (ed) *Encyclopedia of Policy Studies*, New York, Marcel Dekker, pp. 117-155.

Carver, J. (1990), *Boards That Make A Difference: A New Design for Leadership in Nonprofit and Public Organisations*, San Francisco, Jossey-Bass

City of Milwaukee, Wisconsin, (1995), *1996 Proposed Plan and Executive Budget Summary*, Milwaukee, Wis., City of Milwaukee, Department of Administration, Budget and Management Division

Cohen, S. and Brand, R. (1993), *Total Quality Management in Government: A Practical Guide for the Real World*, San Francisco, Jossey-Bass

Cothran, D.A. (1993), 'Entrepreneurial Budgeting: An Emerging Reform?', *Public Administration Review*, 53(5), pp. 445-454

Delivering Better Government: the Second Report to Government of the Coordinating Group of Secretaries (1995), Dublin, Ireland, Government Publications Sales Office

Doig, J.W. and Hargrove, E.C. (eds) (1987), *Leadership and Innovation: A Biographical Perspective on Entrepreneurs in Government*, Md., Johns Hopkins University Press

Eckhert, P., Haines, K., Delmont, T. and Pflaum, A., 'Strategic Planning in Hennepin County, Minnesota: An Issues Management Approach', in J.M. Bryson and R.C. Einsweiler (eds), *Strategic Planning – Threats and Opportunities for Planners*, Chicago, Planners Press 1988; also found in R.L. Kemp (ed), *Strategic Planning for Local Government: A Casebook,* Chicago: Planners Press, 1992; also found in R.L. Kemp (ed), *Strategic Planning for Local Government*, Jefferson, N.C., McFarland, 1993

Elmore, R.F. (1982), 'Backward Mapping: Implementation Research and Policy Decisions', in W. Williams (ed), *Studying Implementation,* Chatham, N.J., Chatham House

Fisher, R. and Ury, W. (1981), *Getting to Yes: Negotiating Agreements Without Give In*, New York, Penguin

Frame, J.D. (1987), *Managing Projects in Organisations: How to Make the Best Use of Time, Techniques and People*, San Francisco, Jossey-Bass

Goggin, M.L., Bowman, A.O., Lester, J.P. and O'Toole, L.J. Jr. (1990), *Implementation Theory and Practice: Toward a Third Generation*, Glenview Ill., Scott, Foresman

Halachmi, A. and Boydston, R. (1991), 'Strategic Management with Annual and Multi-Year Operating Budgets', *Public Budgeting and Financial Management*, 3(2), pp. 293-316

Hammer, M. and Champy, J. (1993), *Reengineering the Corporation*, New York, Harper Business

Hampden-Turner, C. (1990), *Corporate Culture*, Hutchinson, England, Economist Books

Johnson, D.W. and Johnson, F.P. (1994), *Jointing Together: Group Theory and Group Skills* (5th ed), Englewood Cliffs, N.J., Prentice-Hall

Kerr, S. and Jermier, J. (1978), 'Substitutes for Leadership: Their Meaning and Measurement', *Organisational Behaviour and Human Performance*, 22, pp. 375-403

Kingdon, J.R. (1995), *Agendas, Alternatives and Public Policies*, (Rev.ed.) Boston, Little, Brown

Koteen, J. (1989), *Strategic Management in Public and Nonprofit Organisations*, New York, Praeger

Kotter, J.P. and Lawrence, P. (1974), *Mayors in Action*, New York, Wiley

Lipsky, M. (1980), *Street-Level Bureaucracy: Dilemmas of the Individual in Public Services*, New York, Russel Sage Foundation

Lynn, L.E. Jr. (1987), *Managing Public Policy*, Boston, Little, Brown

Manz, C.C. (1986), 'Self-Leadership: Toward an Expanded Theory of Self-Influence Processes in Organisations, *Academy of Management Review*, 11, pp. 585-600

Milward, H.B., Provan, K.G. and Else, B.A. (1993), 'What does the 'Hollow State' Look Like?', in Bozeman, B. (ed), *Public Management: The State of the Art*, San Francisco, Jossey-Bass

Mintzberg, H. (1994), *The Rise and Fall of Strategic Planning*, New York, Free Press

Mitroff, I.I. and Pearson, C.M. (1993), *Crisis Management: A Diagnostic Guide for Improving Your Organisation's Crisis-Preparedness*, San Francisco, Jossey-Bass

Morrissey, G.G., Below, P.J. and Acomb, B.L. (1987), *The Executive Guide to Operational Planning*, San Francisco, Jossey-Bass

National Governors Association (1993), *An Action Agenda to Redesign State Government*, Washington, D.C., National Governors Association

Neustadt, R.E. and May. E.R. (1986), *Thinking in Time: The Uses of History for Decision Makers*, New York, Free Press

Oregon Progress Board (1995), *Oregon Benchmarks, Standards for Measuring Statewide Progress and Institutional Performance*, Salem, Oregon, Oregon Progress Board

Osborne, D. and Gaebler, T. (1992), *Reinventing Government*, Reading, Mass., Addison-Wesley

Peters, T.J. and Waterman, R.H. Jr. (1982), *In Search of Excellence: Lessons from America's Best-Run Companies*, New York, HarperCollins

Pettigrew, A., Ferlie, E. and McKee. L. (1992), *Shaping Strategic Change*, Newbury Park, Calif., Sage

Quinn, J.B. (1980), *Strategies for Change: Logical Incrementalism*, Homewood, Ill., Richard D. Irwan

Randolph, W.A. and Posner, B.Z. (1988), *Effective Project Planning and Management: Getting the Job Done*, Englewood Cliffs, N.J., Prentice-Hall

Roberts, J. (1993), 'Limitations of Strategic Action in Bureaus', in B. Bozeman (ed), *Public Management: The State of the Art*, San Francisco, Jossey-Bass

Roberts N. and Wargo, L. (1994), 'The Dilemma of Planning in Large-Scale Public Organisations: The Case of the United States Navy', *Journal of Public Administration Research and Theory*, 4, pp. 469-491

Rogers, E. (1982), *Diffusion of Innovations*, (3rd ed), New York, Free Press

Sabatier, P.A. (1991), 'Toward Better Theories of the Policy Process', *PS: Political Science and Politics*, 24(2), pp. 144-56

Schein, E.H. (1992), *Organisational Culture and Leadership* (2nd ed), San Francisco, Jossey-Bass

Scriven, M.S. (1967), 'The Methodology of Evaluation', in R.E. Stake (ed), *Curriculum Evaluation, Vol.1: Area Monograph Series on Curriculum Evaluation*, Skokie, Ill., Rand McNally

Senge, P.M. (1990), *The Fifth Discipline: The Art and Practice of the Learning Organisation*, New York, Doubleday

Susskind, L. and Cruikshank, J. (1987), *Breaking the Impasse*, New York, Basic Books

Trist, E. (1983), 'Referent Organisations and the Development of Inter-Organisational Domains', *Human Relations*, 36(3), pp. 269-284.

Wildavsky, A. (1984), *The Politics of the Budgetary Process*, Boston, Little, Brown and Company.

Strategic Management: Choices and Imperatives*

Brendan Tuohy

Introduction

Strategic management is about choices that an organisation wishes to make – choices about its future direction and choices abut the process it adopts. This paper looks at the experience of introducing strategic management into a government department and discusses some of the issues raised and the lessons learned during the process. It also looks at some of the important choices that have to be made by government departments and the imperatives that follow from these choices. Finally, it suggests that some changes in emphasis will be required in organisations in the future.

Part 1: Introducing Strategic Management into the Department of Transport, Energy and Communications

The Department of Energy volunteered to undertake a pilot project in strategic management in 1992 and the process was continued in the newly formed Department of Transport, Energy and Communications

---

* The views expressed in this paper are the author's own views and do not necessarily reflect the views of the Department or the Minister.

in 1993. From the beginning, the objective of the process was to create a durable capability in, and sustainable commitment to, strategic management throughout the department. The management committee drew on the work of Selfridge and Sokalik (1975) which suggests that there are *overt* dimensions to an organisation (e.g. systems, documentation, a planning unit) and *covert* dimensions (e.g. beliefs about change, history and folk-memory of previous attempts at change, fears and feelings of impotency about change) – see Figure 1.

The management committee saw its task more as encouraging a 'change of hearts and minds' than a technical challenge of producing a set of plans for the department. The approach taken was based on the premise that introducing a strategic management process would take some considerable time; it would require a deep and sustainable level of intervention; it would have to put great emphasis on the process and not the documents produced and it would require the ownership of all staff to be fully effective. From an early stage, it became clear that there would have to be a serious concentration on staff training and development and on building up the management support services, if strategic management was to have any real opportunity of taking hold within the department.

The management committee adopted the following definition of strategic management:

> It is a process by which the department maintains a considered and coherent view of likely developments in its internal and external environment in the medium to long term; defines strategic direction and policy objectives; has in place appropriately skilled staff and organisational structures, systems and procedures; develops plans designed to maximise its effectiveness and efficiency in expected circumstances; implements these plans and continually reviews progress, making adjustments, as necessary.

Figure 1
The Organisational Iceberg and Depth of Intervention

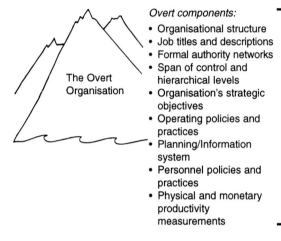

Overt components:

- Organisational structure
- Job titles and descriptions
- Formal authority networks
- Span of control and hierarchical levels
- Organisation's strategic objectives
- Operating policies and practices
- Planning/Information system
- Personnel policies and practices
- Physical and monetary productivity measurements

These components are publicly observable, generally rational, and cognitively derived and oriented to operational and task considerations.

The Overt Organisation

Covert components:

- Emergent power and influence patterns
- Personal views of organisation and individual competencies
- Patterns of interpersonal groups and divisional relationships
- Work group sentiments/norms
- Perceptions of linkages, trust, openness, risk-taking behaviours
- Individual role perceptions and value systems
- Emotional feelings, needs, desires
- Affective relationships between boss and subordinates
- Human resources accounting measurements

These components are hidden, generally affective, and emotionally derived and oriented to the general climate and social/psychological and behavioural/process considerations.

The Covert Organisation

Source: Selfridge and Sokalik, 1975

58

There appear to be as many ideas about what strategic management is as there are people. To help clarify the scope of strategic management, it is proposed to break it into some constituent parts, as follows:

- strategic thinking

- strategic planning and strategy formulation

- strategic implementation (including organisational structures, processes, systems, staff skills, organisational culture, style and values)

- strategic control

- review of the process.

Each of these issues will be discussed in more detail later in the paper. At this stage, I would like to refer to just one concept and that is the idea of 'The Delivery System' for strategy implementation.

'The Delivery System' for Strategy Implementation

In the past, the analysis of issues and prescription have tended to be quite good. The weakest area has tended to be in setting up systems and processes for implementation or delivery of the strategies. Having a good strategy, but without due regard to the support in organisational issues that are required for implementation, has resulted in failure to implement many strategies.

The 'Delivery System' necessary for strategy implementation is a complex, inter-related series of organisational issues that need to be addressed if an organisation is to deliver an effective strategy. They include the issues referred to in Figure 2.

Figure 2

Department of Transport, Energy and Communications
The Delivery System for Stategy Implementation

External Environment

Department Strategy

Financial Resources
- Finance policy and strategy
- Administrative budget
  - greater delegation
  - greater accountability
  - monitoring
- Distribution of resources
- Use of resources
- Audit of resource usage
- Multi-annual projects
- Multi-annual budgets
- Accrual accounting
- Resource budgeting and accounting

Technology (Hard and Soft)
- Location of Dept. HQ and its services
- Complexity and versatility of technology
- Principal working methods including cross-functional operations
- Physical working conditions
- New v Obsolete
- Time-frames (cycles, shifts)
- Computers and communications technology
- Technical capabilities
- Nature of jobs inherent in technology
- IT policy and strategy

Principal Tasks and Processes
- Variety
- Inter-dependability
- Variability
- Aireacht and Executive Tasks
- Work flows, linkages

Management
- Calibre of senior management
- Calibre of middle management
- Calibre of first-line management
- Functioning of the management process
- Attitudes, energy, perspective
- Credibility
- Technical v managerial balance
- Leadership style
- Teamwork
- Management succession

Formal Structures
- Minister as corporation sole
- Differentiation
  - vertical (i.e. no. of layers)
  - horizontal (i.e. no. of divisions/units)
- Job design and team structures
- Grades
- Integration and control
- Distribution of power
- 'In-house' committees
- Linking mechanisms
- Industrial relations structure
- New structures for commercial operations
- Outsourcing
- Linkages to other departments and organisations

Information Organisation
- Values and ideologies
- Quality of relationships
- Symbols of status and trust
- Sense of identity, belonging and equality
- Time management by key people
- Informal power, politics
- General morale, optimism
- Myths, beliefs
- History and traditions
- Attitudes to others
- Work norms

Figure 2 continued

Personnel Policies, Procedures and Industrial Relations	Human Resources	Systems of Measurement and Control	
– Personnel policy	– Number, age, sex, etc.	Cycle of scanning/analysis	Materials
– Recruitment	– Skill mix and potential	Planning	Money
– Induction/socialisation		Resource.Allocation	Labour
– Training and Development	– Economic and social literacy	Measurement re.	Information
– On-the-job		Control	Capacity
– In-house	– Maturity	Information dispersal	Output Volumes
– CMOD	– Attitudes and expectations	Decision making	Quality
– Specialist			Service
– Managerial	– Loyalties		
– Career paths	– Flexibility and versatility		
– Transfer policy			
– CS regulations and conditions			
– New forms of contract		– 'Getting-it-all-together'	
– Performance appraisal		– Total service management	
– Rewards: material, symbolic		– Project management systems	
– Grievance and disciplinary procedures		– Communication system	
– Negotiating procedures (incl. C&A Scheme)		– The political process	
– Department council			
– Superannuation/pensions			
– Manpower planning			
– New agreements			

The Process Adopted

The features of the process adopted by the department include the following:

- Regular off-site meetings of the management committee to discuss strategic management only

- Weekly management committee meetings with circulation of agenda to all staff in advance of the meeting

- Establishment of standing committees, composed initially of principal officers and equivalents, dealing with:

  Personnel
  Training and Development
  Finance
  Information Technology

- Establishment of networks for principals, assistant principals, higher executive officers and administrative officers (subsequently amended)

- Establishment of the Organisation and Development Unit to carry out a training needs analysis and update it; training management support units; delivery of an annual training programme and reporting to the management committee

- Preparation of a Statement of Strategy for the Department incorporating a SWOT analysis (strengths, weaknesses, opportunities and threats)

- Mission, Aims, and Objectives for each division

- Details outlined of future initiatives to advance strategic management in the department

- Introduction of programme reviews, i.e. annual reviews by the management committee for each division's programmes

- Organisational changes
  - Further devolution to the management of Met Eireann and GSI through formal agreements
  - Changes to the organisational structures
  - Mentoring programmes for staff at executive officer level
  - Development of an information technology strategy (completed)
  - Development of a human resources strategy (currently underway)
  - Development of an accrual accounting system for the department (completed)
  - Development of a resource budgeting and accounting system (underway)
  - Proposals for greater participation by staff in the management of the department
- Preparation of an up-dated Statement of Strategy (for publication in September 1996)
- Publication of an annual report (due in July 1996).

The process of strategic management is dynamic and is continuously developing. One of the most interesting projects currently underway is the introduction of structures for greater participation by staff in the management of the department. It is hoped that, through this mechanism, staff will become more involved in the management of the department. It is also expected that the structures and processes for participation will continue to evolve over time.

Initial Questions

Early on in the strategic management process in the department a number of key questions arose. Not only had these to be tackled but they had to be resolved satisfactorily before the process could be continued. Taking time to debate these issues in depth proved later to be critical to the development of an overall confidence with the strategic management process, and to a common understanding amongst senior management of what strategic management actually means. It may be useful to elaborate on these questions.

1. Why undertake strategic management?

The main benefits of undertaking strategic management are as follows:

- It crystallises policy choices.

- It minimises surprises and crises.

- It helps the department to make decisions today in light of their future consequences.

- It ensures a better deal in negotiations.

- It helps to establish priorities and establish the basis of trade-offs among competing agenda items.

- It minimises risk from a piecemeal approach.

- It helps decision making across functions.

- It provides the rationale for winning 'hearts and minds' better in support of long-term benefits that have short-term pain.

- It provides the parameters and direction in which all stakeholders can plan and operate.

- It provides the criterion against which to judge the wisdom of particular initiatives.

2. Whose job is it to do strategic planning?

This issue came up as a fundamental question. Was it not the government's job to develop strategic plans and the civil servants' job to implement such plans as a government had developed? Could it be seen as somewhat undemocratic if civil servants were engaged in strategic planning in areas that government had not yet declared a policy?

I would suggest that it is not only legitimate but imperative for civil servants to undertake strategic planning. The planning process should result in well-thought-out policy options being presented to government, but the final say over which policy is to be followed is always, of course, the government's.

3. What constraints are there on the scope for strategic thinking?

This question is related to Question 2 above in that the government programme, *A Government of Renewal*, is the government's own work programme. This should underpin all policy and must be implemented by civil servants. The programme is not comprehensive in itself and other issues must also be included, though not specifically referred to in the programme. The government must also have the right to amend its programme in light of developments and as the environment changes. It is often the job of the civil service to highlight the changes that are needed and to propose these to government. Therefore, it is incumbent on civil servants to think beyond the specifics of the government programme, and if necessary, to propose amendments to government. The prerogative to amend its programme is always, of course, government's.

4. Is there any point in undertaking a planning process without the guarantee of resources being made available in advance?

This question arose from the frustrating experiences over many years of putting much effort into planning and then being informed that the resources would not be available to implement the plans.

Even though this could always be a likely outcome, there are still major benefits in going through the planning process and putting a well thought-out and coherent strategic plan together. It is far more difficult, for example, for the Department of Finance to dismiss such a plan than to dismiss a poorly thought-out, partial plan and it is easier to get resources for a detailed, comprehensive plan than for a few vague ideas.

5. *Why bother with planning if other departments are not also planning?*

There are many areas of overlapping responsibilities between government departments and there is a need for effective coordinating mechanisms. The costs of not having such effective mechanisms in place are probably quite large. Inevitably this need for coordination will be highlighted and departments will be forced into cooperating with each other. Rather than waiting for such an arrangement to be forced upon us, it is more beneficial for the department to have carried out its own strategic planning, to have identified the possible areas for cooperation and to have begun the process of cooperation in a proactive manner.

6. *Have we the competencies and resources?*

Embarking on any new initiative raises questions about the availability of sufficient resources and competencies to carry through the initiative. In relation to strategic management, while there is a body of knowledge on the general subject, it relates predominantly to the business world. There is a very limited amount of information about strategic management in the public sector and the particular challenges faced by managers in the public sector. It was therefore necessary to seek out specific material that dealt with strategic management in the public sector and to adapt some of the other material to make it relevant. This material was made available to those involved in the strategic management process within the department, thereby helping to develop the competence of existing staff on the subject.

A second issue arose when considering the resources required to implement an effective strategic management process. It became apparent that there would be a need to assign specific resources to the process i.e. not just researching the subject and facilitating the process within the department, but also developing the new systems that are required to support the process within the department. For example, specific staff were assigned to a number of projects such as setting up an accrual accounting system, establishing a training programme, developing a human resource strategy and an information strategy. Asking staff handling day-to-day work to also undertake the establishment of new systems that can operate in parallel with the existing systems is a very difficult task. However, even though there is a major drawdown of resources by establishing teams to develop the new systems, it ensures that the task is completed in a reasonably short time scale and it is a visible sign to the organisation that senior management is committed to the process.

Lessons from the Process

A number of points arose during the process that may be worthwhile noting.

Strategic management as a process

- Strategic management is about changing an organisation. It is a long-term process that demands a great deal of senior management time and energy. It is not just about producing a glossy plan or simply promising better customer service.

- Civil servants are quite happy dealing with documents and their training has tended to put much emphasis on writing things down. But strategic management is not about documents, rather it is about processes and it may take some time for staff to become comfortable with processes as opposed to documents.

- There was a debate for a number of years in the academic journals about which should come first – structure or strategy. From our experience, the relationship is symbiotic in that the initial strategy is a function of the structure in place at the time. Once the initial strategy is being implemented, it is likely that the structure will itself change and this will lead to a new strategy being developed. Therefore, it would appear reasonable to develop a strategy within the existing structure but to include a facility to review both the strategy and the structure.

- There is a need to have periodic reviews or audits of the strategic management process to ensure that it is progressing as planned. We have used an outside facilitator to undertake these reviews. We believe that this helps to present a factual report to management of the state of the strategic management process. It also feeds back comments from staff to management on their perceptions of the process.

Importance of vision

- An integral part of a strategic management is scanning the environment and looking at changes to better position the organisation in the future. The ability to envision and articulate a future and to look from the future back to today, to determine the gap that needs to be closed, is not easy for people and it demands specific training for staff.

The management of change

- Attitudes to change are deeply engrained in staff. These are based on their previous experiences of attempts at change in the public sector and on their perception of the forces (if any) currently driving change. In the main, their previous experiences of attempts at change have been quite negative and these memories still remain.

- Structural obstacles to change exist. These can be in the form of existing structures and processes that are more geared to dealing with (and maybe even protecting) the existing systems and practices than looking at how best the organisation should be organised to carry out its mission.

- It is important that a climate-setting process is established aimed at getting staff to recognise and accept the need for change and the scale of the change required. This can be a very time-consuming process that demands top management time. Staff must buy into the need for change and they must feel that their views are taken seriously.

- Getting staff and managers to articulate the benefits of strategic management can help to gain its acceptance.

- The approach adopted to introducing change is very important. If it is accepted that the most desirable form of change is one in which staff and management see the need for change, are involved in determining the change strategies and are committed to the changes, this will take a long time. It will demand the sustained commitment of senior management and the establishment of appropriate structures and processes for staff participation. This has not been a feature of past efforts at change.

Leadership and management style

- Much of what is written about strategic management refers to the critical importance of leadership for the process to succeed. Our experience would whole-heartedly support this. The three most critical things that top management can give to support the process are time, time and time. To say one is supportive of strategic management but not to follow this up with visible time commitment by listening to staff and managers and engaging in the various activities that make up the strategic management process, will be quickly seen by all for what it is – token commitment. Needless to say, the reaction by staff to such an action is quite predictable.

- Writing mission statements and aims for any organisation may bring one into the lofty realms of pious statements and well-meaning sentiments. The reality for staff is often very different and it is their experience of what happens in the organisation, not what the organisation says in its published aims and values, that is important. Therefore, top management's style of doing business – what it actually sees as important, what it rewards and values, what behaviour it encourages amongst staff, how it treats staff – is critical. This must be consistent with its stated aims and values or the potential for cynicism will be created.

Role of managers

- The involvement of the principal officers and professional equivalents in the process highlighted a number of issues:

    - their previous experience of planning in the civil service had often resulted in much work being done by themselves but with no resulting changes. This tended to colour their initial view of this initiative and it required a sustained effort by both the management committee and principal officers to keep the process moving along;

    - their pattern of work was such that operational matters tended to predominate. This was quite understandable in the environment in which civil servants operate but it requires to be changed;

    - there was a need to bestow legitimacy on managers taking time out to think about strategic issues and to accept that this should be regarded as an activity proper to principal officers

- Three roles were defined for principal officers:

    - strategic role – responsible for developing and overseeing the implementation of a strategy for the sector for which they have responsibility e.g. electricity sector, telecommunications sector;

- architectural role – responsible for putting in place a suitable infrastructure within the department for the delivery of the strategy for the sector e.g. what skill base and competencies are required; what processes are required to develop and implement the strategy?
- managerial role – as head of a division, responsible for the management of that division (including staff development and succession planning) and, as a manager in the department responsible, in a collegiate manner, for management of the department.

Inter-dependent issues that need to be addressed

- Raising expectations of managers and staff about a better way of running the department or of doing business will quickly turn to cynicism if they do not see actual changes on the ground. Many of the issues identified in our department as requiring change were in the management support areas and, in particular, personnel. It became apparent that a number of the issues were inter-dependent (e.g. devolving responsibility for financial and personnel matters requires the prior existence of information systems and requires the training of managers in advance). Some of the issues were outside the control of the department's management, being the responsibility of the Department of Finance with its central role in personnel matters (e.g. recruitment, promotion and remuneration of staff). Issues that can be dealt with quickly and easily should be dealt with quickly, but an eye must be kept on the overall situation to ensure that the approach is coherent.

- The role of the management support units (e.g. personnel, finance, information technology, organisational development, planning, information and library) has tended to be down-played in the past. If strategic management is to succeed, it will mean totally re-vamped roles for these units, with an increased expertise being developed in the various areas and a changing role for the units to one of support, in the form of expertise and advice, to line managers.

An important query arose, across a number of departments, about the application to the public sector of the principles of strategic management (which were initially developed for the world of business). This tended to highlight some of the differences between the private sector and the public sector and the particular obstacles to introducing change in the public sector. I will cover these issues in the next section.

Potential Obstacles to Change in the Public Sector

As in the private sector, there are many potential obstacles to change in the public sector. But there are quite distinct differences between them. The following are some of the potential obstacles:

1. No catalyst for urgent change

Government departments and public sector agencies generally do not collapse, resulting in large-scale job losses, if they fail to provide a service at a reasonable price to the public. There is no 'bottom line' of profit being essential for survival, as in the private sector. Neither is there exposure to the reality of the marketplace; public agencies tend to be monopolies and consumers do not have a choice of suppliers. That sharp focus and awareness of market competitors, that is apparent in most private sector companies, is noticeably missing from the public sector.

2. Attitudes of managers, staff and staff associations

The key question that many managers and staff ask is 'Why change?' The experience of staff is generally such that they perceive that their success in not cooperating with the introduction of major changes in the past, aligned with a similar attitude by many managers, has been validated and they may tend to see current efforts in a similar light.

Many see that the move towards a more business-like approach, based to some degree on New Public Management Theory and similar New Right philosophies, is fundamentally flawed and capable of seriously undermining the traditional public service values of independence, fairness and probity, and similarly affecting, in a negative way, the democratic accountability of ministers to the electorate through the Oireachtas. Likewise, staff associations, that have a very important role in the public service, are particularly concerned with the effects on their own members' working conditions and career prospects.

3. Unclear direction or vision

There tends to be uncertainty at national level, and even at departmental level, about the future vision of the public service. This lack of clarity may act as an obstacle to change in the minds of staff, although clarity can only come through a process of consultation with staff.

4. Structural obstacles

There is a need to assign specific resources to the change process and this is at a time when resources are being cut back generally in the civil service. When changing from an old to a new system, it is essential to keep the two systems in operation simultaneously. This requires resources and some specific skills that may not be currently available in the civil service.

5. Providing the public service with conflicting mandates

The public service is often expected to operate with conflicting mandates. For example, it may be asked to become more commercial yet provide uneconomic services; or it may be asked to provide new services but it may not be supplied with resources. It is often asked to prioritise, but it may find when it endeavours to close down certain services defined as 'non-priority' that it may not be allowed to do so.

6. Ambiguities concerning the role of the public service

Getting the civil service to change itself is only part of the solution. Elected representatives also have a major part to play in the public service. As the relationship between the civil servants and the elected representatives becomes more complex, there is a need to clarify this relationship and to begin to develop new models for the relationship that can handle these growing complexities. For example, the range and complexity of issues handled by government departments, together with the speed at which matters regularly require to be dealt with, often require decisions to be made by officials without the minister's specific prior approval. This is an accepted modus operandi, yet many members of the public still believe that the minister is involved in all decisions and often they expect the reality to reflect their perception.

The move towards greater managerialism and devolution of power to managers could be seen by some as deepening the democratic deficit. If the move in the public service is towards a greater focus on outputs with an expectation that ministers will extricate themselves from the minutiae and be accountable for the broader policy issues only, then the business of the Oireachtas will also have to be looked at. As the political process and the electoral system have a major effect on the behaviour of elected representatives, any effort at reforming the public service must be matched by congruent reforms of the political process.

There are, of course, other obstacles to change in the public sector.

Part 2: Options in Strategic Management

In this part of the paper I would like to discuss in greater detail the elements that were referred to previously as making up strategic management. It is accepted that the elements are totally inter-connected and dependent upon each other and that strategic management is the total process. To enable discussion of the elements, I would like to explore some issues about each of them, including some options that are available to management.

Strategic Thinking

The reasonable man adapts himself to the world; the unreasonable one persists in trying to adapt the world to himself. Therefore all progress depends on the unreasonable man. (Shaw)

The issue of strategic thinking is often overlooked when considering the elements that go to make up strategic management. Yet it is the most fundamental and important part of the whole area of strategy. By strategic thinking I am referring to the quality of the thinking done by managers about their strategic role. It raises such issues as the scope that is given to managers to think about their organisation and its mission, the strategies available to the organisation and the constraints that are imposed on that thinking.

In relation to strategic thinking in the civil service, the following are some of the issues that could be usefully considered:

• Should managers be free to consider any options or should they be constrained in any way? For example, about a specific issue. such as the development of a strategy for a sector, should they limit their consideration solely to implementing what is contained in the government's programme; or should they consider the issue on a much broader basis, where what is in the government's programme would be one of their considerations (albeit a most important one)? Depending on the constraints imposed on managers and the attitude they adopt when drawing up the strategy, the resultant strategy could be quite different. Because of changes in the environment since the government's programme was initially drawn up, and the importance of the link between the

75

strategy and the environment, it would seem to be more appropriate to consider all options when developing a strategy. Giving managers such a freedom, to think in an unconstrained manner, is critical to having good strategic thinking but it may pose some difficulties at the bureaucratic-political interface.

- Should the status quo be accepted or should it be challenged? From the comments by the Co-ordinating group on the First Statements of Strategy submitted by each department in late 1994, it appears that there was not enough questioning of the status quo by departments with the result that the analyses of strengths, weaknesses, opportunities and threats tended towards a past and current view rather than anticipating future circumstances. Any effective strategic thinking must seriously challenge the status quo and the conventional wisdom of the definition of the 'business that the organisation is in'. To fail to do so, is to delude oneself into believing that one is engaged in strategic thinking.

- The mission of any organisation, and its strategies are based on a view of the external environment that can be either static or dynamic. However, in reality the external environment is dynamic and any debate should be about the rate of change. In some cases, for example in the field of telecommunications or information technology, the rate of change in the environment is very rapid and very dramatic. There may be a tendency to base a view of the environment on a static interpretation and this can be fatally flawed, particularly if there are things happening which can have a major effect and one is not even aware of them.

- We may take a view of the future as a projection of the past or we may take it as a discontinuity. Whichever option we choose has implications for the strategy we pursue. Likewise, we can view the future as something out there that already exists, like an island, or we can view it as something capable of being influenced and created and in which we can play a major part. The perspective we adopt will affect our approach to the outcome.

- One of the most important functions of a manager is to ask the right questions. To this end, managers must be encouraged to continually question and to keep changing the framework in which they question. For example, we could ask 'What is the future of the fax machine given its increasing use over the past few years?' On the basis of historical data, there has been major growth in the use of fax and its continued growth could look assured. Alternatively, we could ask a different question, such as 'What is the future of the fax machine as more and more people use the Internet?' Again, look at the effect that fax had on telex; it would not be unreasonable to predict the demise of fax due to the influence of the Internet. Therefore, by changing how the question is framed, we get a very different answer.

- To avoid the phenomenon of 'groupthink' (Irving, 1971), it is important to include people in the process who are prepared to question the approaches being adopted and to question any consensus being arrived at. ('Groupthink' is defined as a tendency for like-minded people within a cohesive group to agree on issues without challenging each other's ideas or realising that the consensus which seemingly emerges may not represent the actual views of the group).

Strategic Planning

Plans are nothing. Planning is everything. (Eisenhower)

Strategic planning is a systematic process whereby an organisation sets about developing and implementing strategies that enable it to achieve its mission and aims and continually clarify these in the light of a changing environment.

Some issues to be considered include the following:

- Whose job is it to do strategic planning? Is it the job of the politicians and government or the civil service? I have already discussed this issue. Suffice it to say that civil servants must be involved in strategic planning but the adoption of any particular plan is a function of government.

- Should strategies be deliberate or should they be let emerge and change over time? The classical approach to strategy development has been to put great emphasis on deliberate strategies (i.e. to choose a specific course of action and to follow it through to completion). Strategy development in the public sector has often tended to place more emphasis on emergent strategies (ie. strategies that emerge and change over time in light of experience). In a changing environment, including a changing political environment, this may be the more pragmatic approach.

- Should strategies be 'top-down' or 'bottom-up'? Top-down strategies may tend to show a greater appreciation of the broader trends in the external environment, but they may also show strong personal biases of top management and may not reflect the actual capabilities of the organisation to deliver on the strategy. Bottom-up strategies may tend to avoid the realities of the changing external environment and to focus more on the details than the broader picture. An effective strategy would benefit from both a top-down and bottom-up approach, but this is not easy to achieve.

- What planning time-frame should be considered when developing strategies? This depends very much on the rate of change in the external environment. For example, in the case of telecommunications or computer-based technology, the planning horizon may be about one to two years whereas for infrastructural investment, such as roads, airports, electricity generation, the planning horizon is likely to be of the order of ten to twenty years.

- Should the emphasis be on the quality of the plans or the process? While the quality of the plans is critical, the quality of the thinking and the discipline associated with planning and implementation is far more important. In the environment in which the public service operates, there may be a tendency to focus on the production of the plan rather than on the planning process and the subsequent implementation and review and updating of the plan. Planning should be seen as an on-going process.

- Should strategies have single or multiple objectives? In the private sector strategies tend to have single objectives (i.e. maximisation of profits) but in the public sector there are many objectives, some of which may be conflicting, e.g. commercial and social roles. It is impossible to avoid strategies having multiple objectives in the public sector.

Strategy Formulation

Every man takes the limit of his own field of vision for the limits of the world. (Schopenhauer)

When formulating strategies a number of issues need to be considered:

- Is there a clear distinction between objectives and existing functions and between strategies and existing activities? Objectives often tend to be stated in terms of functions rather than as concrete outputs or outcomes to be achieved; and there may be a tendency to describe what is being done currently by the organisation rather than what the organisation should be doing in the future.

- Should strategy be easily attained or should it stretch the organisation? There is a dichotomy for organisations when developing strategies. Should the strategy be easily attainable so that its success can help motivate people, or should it stretch the organisation to strive for something that is more difficult to attain? Should strategy be seen as the most effective use of existing resources or as a compelling and bold vision that attracts new resources?

- Should an organisation have one or more strategies? Public sector organisations can have a wide range of functions, many with little or no relationship to each other. It would not be unusual for organisations to have more than one strategy, but they should be congruent with each other.

- Who should be involved in the formulation of strategy? Should it include managers only or should it include all staff? If it should include all staff, what structures should be put in place to enable them to contribute effectively? What prior training do they need to enhance their involvement? What about the involvement of other divisions and departments and external organisations?

- In formulating strategy, what information is required today and what information is likely to be required in the future when the strategy is being reviewed? Is there a difference and, if so, who is going to be responsible for collecting the information required in the future?

Strategy Implementation

We shape our environments, then our environments shape us. (Churchill)

No matter how good a strategy is, it is most likely to be the implementation that will pose the real challenges, particularly in the public service. Some issues to consider are the following:

- Have the key success factors been addressed (i.e. what is crucial to the organisation's success in achieving its mission and aims)?

Are there adequate supporting mechanisms in place for effective strategy implementation?

- Should the organisation begin strategy implementation before having the required resources available or should it await the availability of resources? The resources required for strategy implementation may not be available in the organisation at the start of the process; it may be necessary to factor in the development or introduction of specific skills and competencies into the organisation. Allowing staff the necessary time in their work programme to develop the required skills, while also continuing to deal with the day-to-day workload, can pose difficulties for managers. There may also be difficulties with unions and staff associations in allowing the external recruitment of people with specific skills.

- Is there sufficient commitment by senior management to give the time required for strategic management or is there a belief that, once the process is underway, the time commitment will diminish? Effective strategy implementation demands visible, committed and sustained leadership over a prolonged period of time. The job of strategy implementation should not be seen as the task of one individual but should be embraced by the top management collectively and this collective approach and commitment should permeate down through the organisation.

- Is staff training seen as a cost or an investment by the organisation? Is the budget sufficient and is there an acknowledged commitment to allowing staff time for training or is it considered that, while training is undoubtedly important, there are not sufficient resources available to release staff for prolonged training? Staff development and training are important in strategy implementation and it should be recognised in the strategy itself. Also, time must be factored into the work programmes for staff training related to the strategy. From an organisational viewpoint, training can be seen as a cost or an investment. If strategic management is to mean anything, training should be seen as a worthwhile and essential investment and not just a cost on the organisation.

• Is there a willingness to learn, during the process of strategy implementation, by listening to stakeholders and revising the strategy as appropriate? The process of strategy implementation provides an ideal opportunity for learning and revising the strategy – if management listens to staff and other stakeholders. Failure to do so can result in lost opportunity and may even prove more costly for the organisation in the long term.

Organisational Change Management

The key to managing change is to create enough psychological safety to permit group members to bear the anxieties that come with re-examining and changing parts of their culture. (Schein)

Having determined a strategy, there is then a need to put in place a process to manage the change. Options open to organisations, in this regard, include:

• Should it be a 'Big Bang' or slow process? Should it be participative or coercive? Should it be a secretive or transparent process? Organisations in highly competitive markets that are subject to rapid change, and where the organisation's future is threatened in the immediate future, tend to opt for the 'Big Bang' approach. This is usually coercive and management just tends to tell the workforce what its plans are for the future of the organisation, without much consultation. Where there is a longer time frame available and the sense of imminent collapse is not present, the potential is there to go for a slow, more open and participative process.

- Should the process be centrally driven and uniform across the organisation or should it be more devolved and allowed to develop differently across the organisation? The benefits of driving a change initiative centrally are that there is a greater critical mass that tends to force change on those who are not so willing to change; it may be easier to get sponsorship for the concept of total organisational change and resources may be combined to deal with issues that are common across the organisation, thereby leveraging the most out of the limited resources. Allowing the change initiative to evolve at different paces across the organisation allows for the possibility of greater 'buy in' by all staff, in their own time; it helps to involve managers who see that they have a greater say in the change process; and, it allows the development of solutions that are specific to the problems as opposed to standardised, common solutions to all problems.

- Should the change process be legally driven or behaviourally driven? If the objective of the change strategy is to get major changes introduced into the organisation, the manner in which this is done is important. Without a catalyst for change in the public sector, many may feel that it is necessary to introduce legislation to effect any major changes. Alternatively, others feel that it is not good to introduce legislation to force through change; there will be difficulties at the beginning of any process in determining what the outcome will be – setting the changes into legislation at the beginning can therefore be inhibiting and detrimental.

Strategic Control

A great wind is blowing and that gives you either imagination or a headache. (Catherine II, The Great)

Strategic control refers to the processes and procedures within the organisation to ensure that the strategy is implemented according to plan. It involves the establishment of strategic objectives, strategic programmes and milestones (the specific tasks by which the strategic objectives will be accomplished, together with time scales for their completion) and strategic budgets (the resources to be spent on strategic programmes). Performance under each heading must be monitored. The control system must also identify key assumptions on which the strategy is premised, and track any changes to those assumptions and their performance implications. Some options available to management include the following:

- Set target achievement levels centrally or allow the managers to set them? Allowing managers to set their own targets is preferable but they should be stretched by the centre and they should, where possible, be benchmarked externally.

- Establish a formal, rigid, bureaucratic strategic control process or integrate it into the management processes with a minimum of lengthy reports. There is no value in having a strategic control process that is separate from the management processes and a highly bureaucratic process is wasteful of resources and unlikely to be effective.

- Emphasise the financial or budgetary control over other elements or see strategic control as a balance to financial control? Budgetary control frequently fails to encompass important strategic objectives, particularly non-financial objectives. It pays no attention to long-term goals and objectives and it does not deal with the performance of the organisation against external benchmarks. With the budgetary system and method of financial accounting used in the civil service, strategic control is even more important as an important balance to financial control.

- Some of the tensions that have to be grappled with when looking at the options available are illustrated in Figure 3.

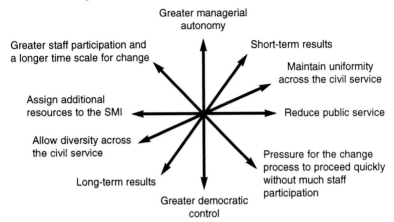

Figure 3. Tensions in Strategic Management

Part 3: Imperatives in Strategic Management

Having looked at some of the elements that go to make up strategic management and having discussed some options open to management, I will endeavour, in this part of the paper, to discuss the imperatives, as I see them, that follow from pursuing specific options.

For example, if specific options are pursued or if particular assumptions are made, there are certain imperatives that follow:

Option/Assumption	Imperative
The objective of the strategic management process is to create a durable capability and commitment to strategic management throughout the whole organisation	The change process will take a long time (maybe five to ten years) and will demand a major investment of resources in training and development both at central level and at department level and a commitment of resources at both levels to maintain the process.
The change process should involve staff at all levels in a structured way.	Effective processes for staff participation will be required both at departmental level and at central level. Managers, staff and staff associations/unions must also learn new approaches and skills so that they can participate effectively.
The rate of introducing change will differ throughout the organisation and, in the case of the civil service, across departments.	A uniform centralised approach to change management must allow for departments to move at different speeds.
Strategic thinking should be unconstrained and should challenge the status quo.	Creative and knowledgeable thinkers, who do not feel constrained in their thinking or afraid to challenge consensus, should find an encouraging environment in their organisation and should be included in teams developing and implementing strategies.
The future is a discontinuity and is a social construct. The external environment is dynamic and the mission and aims of the organisations should reflect this	Departments' strategies should be based on a dynamic view of the future and should seek to be proactive and influence the shape of the future. The mission and aims of departments should challenge the conventional wisdom concerning the definition of the 'business' they are in.

Option/Assumption	Imperative
The civil service should undertake strategic planning and it should be an on-going process that involves staff and produces medium to long-term plans (with multiple objectives) which evolve and change over time.	A strategic planning process, involving staff throughout the organisation, should be integrated into the management routines. This process should extend across the civil service and cater for the various linkages between departments.
Strategic management should have top management commitment; it should emphasise devolution and involve a far greater degree of 'letting go' than in the past and it should encourage targets and objectives to be set by managers but stretched by the centre.	Top management must be seen to be committed and must lead through example by • putting time into the strategic management process over a prolonged period • 'letting go' and devolving to managers while, at central level, stretching the targets that the managers have set for themselves • putting in place a management infrastructure within the department • emphasising the importance of leadership, developing leadership skills amongst managers and rewarding good leaders • focusing more on organisational issues and sponsoring innovation throughout the organisation.

Option/Assumption	Imperative
The current organisational structures and supporting structures are not capable of delivering the strategies required for the future.	There must be a congruence between organisational structure and mission and this requires a re-think of the current approach to maintaining uniform civil service structures. These may not be capable of handling the differences and complexities of an evolving civil service. New structures must be devised so that they can sustain and support the diversity of form required in the civil service.
The roles of central departments need to be re-defined.	There must be a new balance of power at the centre of government with a new role for central departments (Taoiseach and Finance) that places less emphasis on detailed control and more on strategic control and providing leadership, advice and support to line departments while also handling cross-departmental issues.
There needs to be agreement on the future vision of the public service.	The process needs discussion of the issues between all those involved in the public sector inlcuding, in particular, senior management and politicians.
The current relationship between the civil service and the political process is not capable of handling the issues with which it has to deal. There are often particular difficulties with the time horizons where the political process may tend to focus more on the short-term whereas many issues require a longer time horizon	A new relationship between the civil service and the political process must be devised so that democratic accountability is maintained while the necessary managerial autonomy is allowed. This should also allow for a mixture of short-term and long-term planning horizons.

Having discussed some of the options open to decision makers and some of the imperatives that come from pursuing these options, I would now like to conclude by looking at what I consider will be features of organisations of the future.

Part 4: The Organisation of the Future

Prediction is very difficult, especially about the future. (Bohr)

It is not possible to predict exactly what type of organisations will exist in the future. It is quite feasible, though, to look at some of the likely trends and to predict how they might influence the evolution of organisations, particularly in the public sector.

From stovepipes to networks

The traditional government department, and even government itself, is structured along functional, steep hierarchical lines. In recent years, more and more issues are spanning the responsibilities of individual departments and new structures are being put in place to deal with the situations that arise. For example, the drugs problem does not neatly fall into the responsibility of any one government department. It spans the Departments of Justice, Health, Education, An Garda Síochána, Revenue Commissioners and a multitude of other agencies. Dealing effectively with the issue requires a different type of structure than the traditional one which has evolved from the existing structures. Other issues exist that require a response that recognises that there is more than one agency with responsibility in that area (e.g. environmental matters, child-care and taxation are all issues that affect many departments and agencies).

The increasing sophistication of computer systems will also make it easier in the future to provide similar information across a number of organisations simultaneously, thereby helping to underpin and change the relationship to a network structure.

From certainty to uncertainty

As the external environment changes rapidly and the degree of complexity and uncertainty increases, there is need to adjust the strategies we adopt if they are to continue to remain relevant. In the past, the degree of change was not as much as it is likely to be in the future, and therefore the certainty associated with projections of the future will have to give way to a more fluid and uncertain view. There is also a need to change the approach that we have to staff training and development. We need to move from the approach where we see the transfer of knowledge as the key element to one that is based on developing individuals in such a way that they can continuously adjust to a changing environment and feel happy about this.

From looking towards the past to looking towards the future

A key feature in an organisation that is strong on analysis is often an over-emphasis on past performance (e.g. financial performance) as an indicator of likely success in the future. If it is accepted that the future is becoming less and less a projection of the past and more of a discontinuity, then the over-emphasis on past performance can be misleading. There will be a requirement to postulate what the future environment is likely to be and to consider how the organisation is likely to perform in that environment and what things must be got right for that to happen.

From reactive to influencing

The future is not an island out there to be reached. The future is a social construct that is created by people who exist today. If an organisation has a view of what it would like to see, and if its managers are enthusiastic about making this a reality, they can influence decisions and general thinking to help make it happen. If they do not hold a view of the future or they do not consider that they can influence things, then they find themselves in a reactive mode where those who do have a view of the future are seeking to have that view implemented.

From a learning to a listening organisation

There has been much emphasis in recent years on the importance of organisations becoming 'Learning Organisations' whereby they are driven by a vision of the future; they continuously evaluate what they are doing and how they are doing it and they empower their staff, seeing them as the major ingredient of the success of the organisation. The most difficult part of this appears to be getting management in organisations to listen to staff, and it is this ability to listen that will be the hallmark of successful organisations of the future.

Future organisation in the Department of Transport, Energy and Communications

In keeping with the ideas outlined above for the organisation of the future, I will hazard a guess at some possible changes that may occur. I might add that the views are my own personal views.

I see the department shrinking in size as some of its functions are transferred to a new Public Utilities Commission which will be responsible for the regulation of transport, energy and communications sectors. The department will be likely to continue to maintain its role in respect of the development of the sectors and its shareholder role in respect of the state bodies under its aegis.

I see it having a very different structure to what is has today. It will be related to its mission and aims and it will have a great flexibility to respond to changes in the external environment. It will have a much more team-based approach to dealing with issues and these teams will often be cross-departmental. The divisions that provide services other than policy advice may be executive agencies.

Managers will be responsible for managing their divisions and for ensuring that their targets are met. Their targets will be published and they will be accountable through the department's annual report and through Oireachtas committees. They will have much more managerial autonomy, particularly in respect of budgets and staffing, including the facility to hire the staff they require and to have a say in the salaries paid to their staff. Staff will also have an opportunity to move across departments and to seek out specific job opportunities and training opportunities. They will be able to leave the civil service and to return at any level as there will be some facility for open recruitment at all levels.

There will be a process for staff participation at department and at central civil service levels. This will be seen to be effective and will not take from the normal industrial relations machinery. There will be local bargaining at departmental level with facilities for negotiations on a wide range of issues.

The expertise required in such areas as personnel, finance, information technology and information/library will be developed or specially recruited and these support units will work closely with line managers and departmental top management. Staff in those units will be recognised as experts.

A forum for discussion of public management issues will be available through a joint committee involving both elected and appointed public servants.

Conclusion

The introduction of strategic management into the public service is a challenge for all involved – staff, management, elected representatives and all others with a stake in the public service. It will be a long process and, by adopting a proactive approach, as the Strategic Management

Initiative is endeavouring to do, it offers an opportunity for real ownership and participation by all – provided suitable structures and processes are put in place for it to happen. Fundamental questions need to be asked and choices need to be made. But, once specific options are pursued, then certain imperatives follow. To endeavour to pursue the options without implementing the imperatives, is not a recipe for success. It is to be hoped that the will and commitment will be available to pursue both the desired options and the imperatives that flow from these.

References

Irving, James (1971), 'Groupthink', *Psychology Today*

Selfridge, R.J. and Sokalik, S.L. (1975), *A Comprehensive View of Organisation Development, MSK Business Topics*, Winter edition.

Strategic Management:
Choices and Imperatives

A response to Brendan Tuohy
Frank Ryan

Brendan Tuohy's paper gives a very comprehensive and stimulating overview of the implications of strategic management for the civil service. I am particularly struck by his insight that if we pursue specific options, as the strategic management process impels us to do, there are then certain imperatives that arise from following these options. These imperatives must be addressed if strategic management is to take root.

In the first part of my response, I highlight some of the issues that seem to me to be of particular importance arising from Brendan's paper. In the second half, I draw on some of my own experiences of facilitating the introduction and development of strategic management to raise some points of concern regarding the SMI process.

Key issues in strategic management

The definition of strategic management adopted by the Department of Transport, Energy and Communications starts off by saying: 'It is a process ....' I believe that this emphasis on the process is correct. Strategic management is not about producing glossy plans that sit on shelves gathering dust. It is about evolving a process whereby strategic issues are identified and procedures and systems put in place to address those issues. This is not to say that plans do not have their role. Of course they do. Plans can be important in translating thinking into action and ensuring that the process has an impact. But it is the process that is the driving force of strategic management, not the plans – they are by-products.

Associated with this idea of strategic management as a process rather than plan, in the public service it is important that strategic management encourages a *corporate approach* to the management of strategic issues. It is not about amalgamating disused plans and coming up with a collection of strategies based on divisional analyses. To be successful, strategic management must address the corporate dimensions of a department, office or agency's work, and then see how the issues that arise can best be addressed at divisional level.

It is also important, as I mentioned at the beginning, and as Brendan Tuohy's paper states, that strategic management be seen as being about putting an emphasis on the *choices* that an organisation makes. And associated with the concept of choice is that of *priorities*; choice implies deciding what should receive high priority and what should not. This brings in the political dimension to strategic management in the public service: choice and priorities are ultimately decided as part of the political process. But as Tuohy rightly illustrates in his paper, civil servants must be able to put options to government for their consideration, and not be constrained by specific programmes. The final choices are rightly government's, but a deep-rooted strategic management process must encourage departments themselves and public servants more generally to think about the range of options and priorities that they should be addressing. Strategic management must encourage a long-term view, and help ensure that short-term decisions are compatible with this view.

Another key point made in Tuohy's paper is that there must be a review of the process. Review is needed to ensure that the strategic management process is operating as it should: are key issues being addressed; are staff 'buying-in' to the process; are the necessary organisational changes being made? For such a review to be successful, a number of issues must be addressed:

- The review should not be seen as a 'once-off' or series of 'once-off' exercises.

- Strategic review should be on-going, with periodic reviews of progress both of the overall approach and of the tackling of key strategic issues.

- Crucially, the review process must be integrated into the day-to-day management and decision-making of departments, offices and agencies. It should not be seen as a separate exercise, but as part of the feedback loop on strategic issues.

Having said all this, it must be recognised that the SMI is not a panacea for all government ills. If tackled and taken seriously, the SMI will raise hard questions about how Ireland is governed. Tuohy indicates some of the fundamental issues to be addressed: how to encourage ownership and participation; how to link the process with resource allocation; defining the respective roles of politicians and civil servants; getting the balance between devolution and central control. The SMI will surface these issues if it does its job well, but will not of itself solve them. It must be part of a broader agenda of change in the civil and public service.

Lessons learnt from personal experience

Having outlined some of the key issues that struck me from Tuohy's paper, I would also like to raise a number of issues that seem to me to be crucial to the successful development of SMI, based on my own experience of acting as a facilitator for a number of government departments and offices and local authorities.

Firstly, staff are a key and vital resource. This may sound like a platitude, but it is an issue we ignore at our peril. Staff, particularly front-line staff, have a wealth of experience and insights without which strategic management can only ever be a partial success. Involving staff, and encouraging their views on the identification and tackling of strategic issues is a central challenge for the SMI process.

It must also be recognised that the SMI represents a significant challenge to existing organisational culture in the civil and public service. Strategic management as a process implies greater attention being paid to participation and collaboration. Such attributes can sit uneasily beside the more traditional values of hierarchy and bureaucracy. The culture of public service organisations must evolve, with greater attention being given to openness and, in particular, to valuing users' views of the service. Strategic management puts significant emphasis on assessing user's needs and views, and this presents particular challenges for the public service.

Linked to the existing culture is a tendency to accept the status quo in many organisations. Yet, strategic management challenges this perspective, and asks us to develop a vision of what things should be like, giving a future focus to activities rather than concentrating solely on existing activities. We cannot merely project the past and the present into the future. The challenge is to match these imperatives with an openness to explore new ways of working and tackling the central issues of our time.

There are two particular issues which my experience of facilitation indicates that we need to address as the SMI takes root and is broadened out to the wider public service:

- how to ensure coordination between the various strategies produced by the many public service organisations that exist. Encouraging such coordination without becoming overly bureaucratic in our structures will be a major challenge;

- how to develop and use appropriate performance indicators that tell us if we are getting it right. At the moment, we are not so good at measuring whether strategies are successful. Strategic management challenges us to develop measures and indicators that enable judgements to be made on how the process is working.

I have concentrated on the challenges and issues I see arising out of SMI. Not in any negative sense. Strategic management, as Brendan Tuohy has so clearly illustrated, has the potential when done well to radically improve the way the public service works, both for users and for staff. But if it is to do this, we must not shirk from the challenges that arise from the strategic management process. It is only by tackling them that the hoped-for benefits will fully materialise.

Devolving from the Centre: The UK Experience

Colin Talbot

Introduction

In 1988 the UK government accepted a report, the Next Steps report, which recommended transforming the structure of the civil service (Jenkins et al 1988). The executive functions of government (delivering services, collecting taxes, regulating, enforcing and researching) as distinct from the policy formation functions (supporting ministers) were to be restructured into executive agencies. Each Next Steps Agency, as they became known, would have a named chief executive (CE), accountable directly to ministers, and a 'policy and resources framework' giving it a clear focus and targets. Almost three-quarters of the UK's 'home civil service' have now been transferred to such agencies. The transition process is illustrated crudely in Figure 1.

Next Steps attempts to solve the 'policy' dominance problem by creating a new breed of managers and organisational structures which concentrate on service and programme delivery, not policy. The intended separation was between policy management (departmental centre) and operations management (agencies) with *both* being directly accountable to ministers. This is what could be called the 'apartheid option' – separate but equal development of policy and operations

Figure 1: Creating Executive Agencies

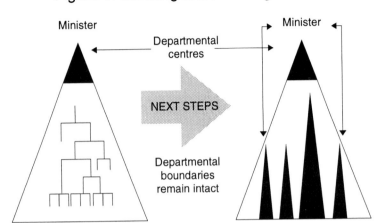

management within the civil service. More recently UK ministers have introduced a second, and very different, notion: ministers are responsible for policy and agency CEs for operations. This was not the original intention of Next Steps. Nor is it consistent with the actual relationship between ministers and agency CEs.

One important point to note is that agencies have not breached departmental boundaries. This has important implications for the real status of agencies vis-à-vis departmental centres.

Recent evidence has clearly demonstrated that there is a great deal of variation in how the control and reporting mechanisms for agencies are operated in practice. Some have tended to imply that the degree of variation relates primarily to their individual ministers' predilections. While this is undoubtedly a factor (and life would be very dull if personalities did not affect such issues) there are wider issues involved than ministerial quirks. The critical factors probably have more to do with the nature of agencies themselves and the systems, rather than the personalities by which they are controlled and held to account. Before going further it is therefore worth trying to get a more concrete picture of what we mean when we talk about 'executive agencies'.

The Variability and Viability of Agencies

One of the points stressed in the original Next Steps report was that the civil service engaged in a great many diverse activities and that these needed similarly diverse structures, management and systems to match the 'job to be done' (Jenkins et al 1988).

The creation of agencies has certainly led to a greater diversity of organisational units, although how far it has led to diversity in systems management and culture is another question. In some cases (e.g. Social Security) the design of new organisational structures as a result of the creation of agencies seems to have been both structurally and culturally significant. In others (e.g. the Home Office) the changes seem to have followed pre-existing structures and the resulting degree of structural and cultural change seems to have been far less. In even more extreme examples the pre-existing organisational unit which has been redesignated an 'agency' was already a non-ministerial department (e.g. Royal Mint). There is a very real sense in which some of the 'agencification' programme has been more about 're-badging' existing structures than creating radically new ones, something which the Next Steps project manager has specifically rejected.

There are a number of other ways in which agencies vary. Size (both absolute and relative) is one key variable. The majority of agencies are small. Most discussions of agency size focus on staffing. The majority of agencies are quite small in staffing terms:

*   11 have less than 100 staff (the commonly accepted definition of 'small enterprises')

*   41 have less than 500 staff ('small and medium enterprises' (SMEs))

*   63 have less than 1,000 staff, and

*   76 have less than 2,000 staff.

However, these small agencies account for only about one-third of the people working in agencies. Two-thirds of agency staff work in a handful of 'super' agencies – Benefits, Employment, Prisons, Customs and Excise and Inland Revenue.

Agencies' roles vis-à-vis their departments and ministers also vary enormously. For example, the Prison Service accounts for over 70 per cent of its department's staffing but for only 26 per cent of its spending. In some departments, agencies account for the bulk of what it does in both staffing and expenditure terms (e.g. Social Security). In others, agencies may account for neither many staff nor for much in the way of spending (e.g. Health).

Any agency is of course potentially a source of political embarrassment to ministers but some are inherently more newsworthy than others – a serious prison break-out, for example, caused far greater public controversy than a serious blunder in the Forensic Science Service (both Home Office agencies). Small and politically 'insensitive' agencies are unlikely to get much real attention from ministers, whatever their formal status may be.

One issue which has arisen is whether or not such small organisations are really viable entities in a public services context, especially with all its informational, audit and control demands to satisfy public accountability requirements.

Recent moves, such as the creation of the Defence Evaluation and Research Agency (DERA) (11,248 staff) by merging the Defence Research Agency (8,770), the Chemical and Biological Defence Establishment (620) and the Defence Operational Analysis Centre (160), also suggest a reconsideration of what constitutes a viable agency. The chief executive of the new DERA has stated that the primary reason for the merger was to achieve 'economies of scale' and it is clear such an argument might well apply elsewhere.

The recent inclusion of a requirement to consider 'rationalisation or merger' as part of the agency 'prior options' review process tends to support this view (Office of the Public Service 1995). However there is clearly an obstacle to achieving this where similar functions, which might be better managed together, currently fall within different departmental boundaries or even elsewhere in the public sector. No Next Steps agency has been established which breaches departmental walls, nor is there any evidence of this even being considered.

Control and Governance Arrangements

The original intention of the Next Steps programme was that each agency would have:

> ... a policy and resources framework set by a department ... These units, large or small, need to be given a well defined framework in which to operate, which sets out the policy, the budget, specific targets and the results to be achieved ... The framework will need to be set and updated as part of a formal annual review with the responsible minister ... (Jenkins et al 1988).

The intention was thus to have a single annually agreed, 'policy and resources' framework document. Such a single, simple, framework would have clear advantages in the strategic management of executive functions within government. It never happened. Policy and resources remained separate, with agency framework documents setting out policy, objectives and responsibility issues but *not resources or performance* (they also became three-year, and later five-year documents rather than annual). Resources continued to be managed via the departmentally based Public Expenditure Survey (PES) system. *Performance* became the subject of an annual agreement over 'key performance indicators' (KPIs).

Far from there being a clear, simple, 'policy and resources' framework for each agency, an extremely complex web of systems and resulting documents have evolved, as is illustrated by the listing below, which is only a partial list of the most important systems/documents used to provide direction and control for agencies:

- Framework Document (5 years)
- PES plan (1-3 years)
- Business Plan (1 year)
- Corporate Plan (3 year)
- Efficiency Plan (1-3 years)
- Key Performance Indicators (1 year)
- Charter Standards (?)

There is a great deal of overlap between these documents and systems, with objectives, resources and performance for each agency set or implied in a variety of different forms and systems.

This would not be problematic if some coherence and consistency had been maintained across a range of systems. Unfortunately, this seems to have proved impossible to achieve. Serious dysfunctions and dysfunctional elements have emerged in the practice of the strategic management of agencies.

Also these controls are employed by different organisations, as Figure 2 illustrates.

Figure 2: Mapping and Controls

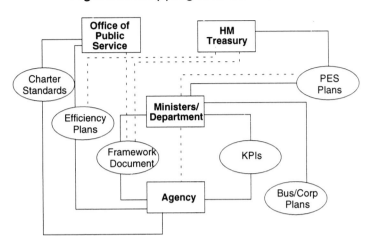

The diagram in Figure 2 tries to capture some of the main levers being employed in the strategic management of agencies. As can be seen, the levers are complex and driven by different actors in the system. Moreover, this diagram is a simplification of an even more complex process. For example, it ignores the very real differences which may emerge between ministerial and departmental perspectives on agencies and the 'filtering' role which departments play as gatekeepers between ministers and agencies.

This raises a key question as to who manages strategy? As the system of the strategic management of agencies has evolved, a number of devices have been introduced to try to 'patch up' some of the problems:

- The problem of ministers being entirely dependent on senior departmental officials for advice about agencies' frameworks, resources and targets has been addressed through the introduction of 'Ministerial Advisory Boards' (MABs), which include external advisors. It is unclear how well this has worked.

- Within departments the lack of strategic coordination of departmental relationships with agencies has been addressed through the establishment of the so-called 'Fraser Figure', a kind of chief coordinator. Departments have also, in many cases, introduced departmental boards, with mixed results.

- At the agency level some have tried to increase strategic management effectiveness by the introduction of agency boards, including external non-executive directors.

These arrangements are illustrated graphically (in part) in Figure 3.

Figure 3: Governance Arrangements

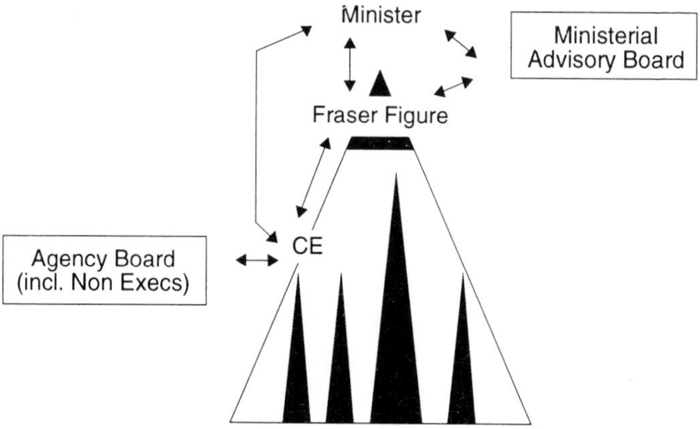

The possible confusion within this system is self evident. The case of the Prison Service and the sacking of Derek Lewis is a case in point. Most of the external non-executive directors resigned in protest against Lewis's dismissal on the grounds that the Prisons Board had carried out strategy which had been agreed with ministers.

To summarise, initially a simple relationship between ministers and agencies was envisaged; one of the foundations of the Next Steps was that chief executives would be directly accountable to a minister in a 'quasi-contractual' relationship. In reality, this simple relationship has failed to materialise. The 'quasi-contractual' relationship is confused and confusing, with a wide range of different documents and decision systems in play; lack of clarity (and consistency in practice) about ministers' roles; variable levels of interest; variable levels of real structural change; etc.

While there have been some improvements and there is at least now a framework which can be more openly discussed, the overall impression is one of poor implementation and weak continuing management of the 'agencification' process.

The Performance of Agencies

The original purpose of the Next Steps changes was not, as some now allege, to separate ministers' responsibility for policy making from operational responsibility of managers. The aim of Next Steps was rather to separate two different forms of management – policy management (departments) and operational management (agencies) – both of which would be directly accountable and responsible to ministers.

It is easy to forget that this was not an aim in itself, but was meant to help 'improve management in government' by creating a new emphasis on the management of operations, free from the shackles of policy-dominated departments. This in turn would, it was hoped, lead to substantial efficiency improvements which could either be realised as economies (reduced spending) or more effective services (including quality improvements), or both.

The crucial question here is: has a new system of improved operational management been created by the Next Steps process? Has this in turn led to improvements in efficiency? The answer is : we do not know. The reason that we do not know is that the current system of measuring, monitoring and accounting for agency performance is quite inadequate to the task.

The disjointed system of strategy making has produced the type of confused pattern in linking organisational aims and objectives to performance targets set out in Figure 4 below.

Figure 4: Objectives and KPIs

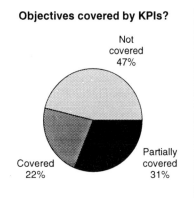

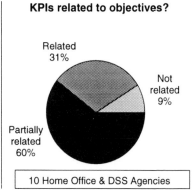

This situation, of objectives being only partially covered by key performance indictors (KPIs) and many KPIs only partially related to objectives, was specifically criticised in the recent Learmont Report (1995) on the problems of the Prison Service. For example, one of Learmont's criticisms was the failure to incorporate into the Prison Service's KPIs any target in relation to staff development, despite this being one of the service's values and one of seven strategic priorities. There has also been conflicting advice and guidance on performance, as the following quotations, taken from the same page of a document offering advice on the Strategic Management of Agencies (Office of the Public Service 1995) illustrates:

> Targets should form a balanced package covering the dimensions of output, time, quality and cost.
> *or*
> Targets should generally be focused on outputs rather than inputs. They should be concerned with what managers achieve with their resources, not with measuring those resources.

The first quotation clearly recommends that a balanced set of measures of performance is needed which includes outputs *and inputs* (costs). The second suggests an emphasis only on outputs. In fact, most agency KPIs have focused *only on outputs* (about 68 per cent) and only a minority measure inputs (14 per cent) or efficiency (13 per cent). Many agencies only measure outputs.

Such advice, and the fact that the population of agencies changes year on year, that individual KPIs and targets have changed year on year, that global figures are unweighted, and that there is no auditing of KPI information, make the claims for year-on-year improvements in the performance of agencies highly debatable.

The degree of lack of comparability, year on year, is graphically illustrated in the 1995 annual Next Steps review (1996) which attempts an analysis of KPIs over time. It concludes that of around 1,400 KPIs reported for 1995, only about 500 can be compared with the previous year's data because the KPIs had either changed so much or were non-quantifiable. The comparisons which were possible provide some startling evidence. Of the 500 KPIs for 1995 which were compared to the same set for 1994, nearly half were set at levels which were actually lower than the previous year's outturn (see Figure 5).

Figure 5: Increasing Performance?

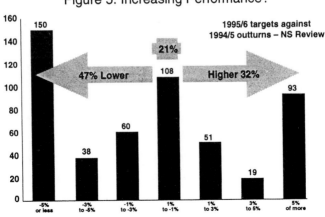

Finally on performance, it should be noted that one of the first curiosities of the performance measurement systems developed for agencies is the diverse range of the number of KPIs felt adequate to monitor individual agencies. On average, agencies have about seven KPIs each, although these range from one KPI (Royal Mint) to twenty-one KPIs (Customs and Excise).

The Royal Mint's single KPI is 14 per cent average current cost return on assets per year. It is difficult to believe that this minimalist approach to performance management can capture the real richness of the Royal Mint's objectives. Its 1990 Framework Document sets out four objectives including return on sales; meet key objectives; maintain high quality work; and put the customer first. It also goes on to talk about a set of ten strategic and business objectives which are set out in the four-year Corporate Plan (which is not publicly available). None of these objectives are reflected in the single KPI, except perhaps by what might be inferred from performance on this single measure.

At the other end of the spectrum some agencies have complex and detailed sets of KPIs. Customs and Excise, for example, have a well-linked and structured set of KPIs which give a balanced view of performance across the organisation (Customs and Excise 1995).

Relationships Between Departments and Agencies

One consequence of the small size of many agencies is the relatively low grade of many agency CEs in terms of the senior civil service. One agency chief executive described having met the relevant secretary of state only twice: once at an official function and once to discuss a specific issue. Another chief executive openly described a Grade 3 in the parent department as 'my boss' and stated that they had virtually no access to ministers; that which did occur was mainly regulated by departmental officials. As an illustration, it was graphically described how specific proposals, from the CE, on the future of the agency had been substantially altered by departmental officials before being submitted to ministers.

This is hardly surprising given that on current figures, of 115 agency chief executives appointed, eighty-three (72 per cent) are career civil servants. They are likely to see their career, past and future, in terms of their relationships with their colleagues, especially senior colleagues. In numerical terms, agency chief executives make up less than 4 per cent of the new senior civil service. Most of this small band are graded in the lower ranks of the new senior civil service. For every career civil service agency CE at Grade 5, there are over 2,000 posts at the same grade to which she or he may be posted and over 800 more senior posts (and colleagues) to which they might aspire (or wish to gain favour with). Given that civil service promotion relies heavily on peer and superior assessments of the ability and merit of individuals, it is unlikely that career civil service CEs are going to be 'advice resistant' when 'guidance' is offered by their more senior colleagues in departments.

The reality of power relations and career prospects between 'operational' managers in agencies and 'policy' managers in department centres was best illustrated by information revealed in the Oughton Report on career management. This revealed that it was expected that some 90 per cent of the old 'senior open structure' grades (1-3) would remain in department centres – with only 25 per cent of civil service staff – whilst only 10 per cent would be working in agencies – with 75 per cent of the staff.

Any career civil servant wishing to reach the highest echelons of the service could clearly make a very simple calculation about the relative merits of 'operational' versus 'policy' management.

The primacy of 'policy' management was also confirmed by the review of the so-called 'fast stream' recruitment and training programme. The report stressed that the 'fast stream' was, and should continue to be, focused on developing the future policy managers for departmental centres and suggested, rather honestly, changing the name to 'policy management programme'. The government found this change too explicit and, whilst accepting all the other recommendations of the report declined the new label. Whatever the 'name of the rose', the programme was and clearly remains about policy management.

But what of the impact on central departments of agencies? It is noteworthy that until the requirement for senior management reviews (SMRs), set out in the White Paper *Continuity and Change*, few departmental centres had registered significant structural or managerial changes as a result of Next Steps. In some cases this was clearly justified, in the sense that Next Steps agencies by themselves represented a fairly small structural change to the overall work of the department. In others, the need for change was more transparent.

The seriousness with which SMRs were conducted showed wide variations ranging from:

conducted by the Permanent Secretary, PFO and Director of Establishments (MAFF); to,

conducted by a Grade 5, plus a small team and external advisors (Home Office)

However there have been significant reductions in senior management in departments in the last couple of years, as Figure 6 illustrates.

Figure 6: Reducing Senior Management

Treasury	25%
Trade and Industry	27%
MAFF	25%
Environment	29%
Home Office	24%
Welsh Office	15%
Education and Employment	30%
Social Security	27%

From 1st April 1994 baseline

These reductions are obviously significant; however, there is an element of 'double counting' because some posts had already gone before senior management reviews took place. And, the degree of variation in reductions does not match the degree of variation in senior management responsibilities across departments, measured by some crude indicators such as senior managers/staff ratio; senior managers/programme expenditure ratio; etc.

Conclusions

The conclusion of this analysis has to be that the impact of agencies in the strategic working of senior management and individual senior managers has been at best patchy.

The existing system of providing public information about existing agencies' performance does not provide the basis for any meaningful judgements to be made. It also raises serious doubts about the claimed improvements in performance as a result of Next Steps. While the volumes of data available have increased, in many ways its comprehensibility and utility has decreased. We certainly do not yet have a system of monitoring the performance of executive agencies which would satisfy minimum requirements for assessing economy, efficiency and effectiveness, never mind more sophisticated approaches. To reverse a popular phrase, in this case it may be that 'more is less'.

The crucial question is, why? What started out as an attempt to create a single, simple, framework for agencies which would have aided public accountability has resulted in a complex web of controls and reporting regimes which has little of the clarity originally envisaged.

Next Steps can be seen as a product of the 'new managerialism' (Pollitt 1991) or the 'new public management' (Hood 1991). Despite all the internal inconsistencies of these approaches, the general thrust of desegregation of organisational units, managerial devolution and performance target setting are clearly consistent with the original intentions of Next Steps.

Whitehall was characterised as a 'village culture' twenty years ago by Heclo and Wildavsky (1974). Recent evidence suggests that whilst forms have changed, the essential relationships at the top of the civil service have not changed appreciably.

Flynn (following Ouchi's theory (1981) of clans, hierarchies and markets) has suggested that the UK civil service can be viewed as a 'clan' sitting on top of a 'hierarchy' (1994). This view is consistent with Helclo and Wildavsky's 'Whitehall Village'. In their village there were closely linked communities or families, grouped around the Treasury, the Cabinet Office and the spending departments. The analysis presented above suggests that Next Steps has been absorbed into this culture and may even have exaggerated the differences between the Whitehall Village or clan on the one hand and the bureaucratic machine culture of the executive functions on the other. Indeed, the creation of the new senior civil service can be seen as the explicit surfacing of a defined and delineating village/clan membership.

The 'new managerialism' or 'new public management' may be viewed by the Whitehall villagers as a 'good thing' for executive agencies but not appropriate to their more collegial, congenial, culture. The inconsistencies and contradictions in the systems of agency management by Whitehall identified above are entirely explicable within such a theoretical framework.

The evidence of the extremely weak and disjointed system(s) for setting performance targets for agencies suggests that little real attention is being paid to the 'corporate management' role of departmental centres. Figure 7 illustrates the roles which departmental centres can fulfil.

Figure 7: Roles of the Departmental Centre

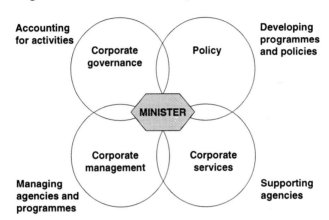

This model is a slightly more complex representation of the traditional 'policy-administration' paradox in public services; policy and administration are separable in concept but not in practice.

Unlike private sector corporations, ministries and departments will inevitably tend to have larger 'cores' because of their *policy* and *governance* roles. The problematic issue has always been that the latter roles have always tended to dominate senior managers' concerns to the exclusion of corporate *management* and *services*.

The origins of the UK's Next Steps programme lay in the perceived need to find a mechanism to give a new importance to *managing* programmes and services. The solution was executive agencies. The evidence so far is that it has only partially worked and that there are a whole host of problematic issues which need addressing before it can be termed a success.

The Way Forward

This paper suggests that, whilst there have been undoubted improvements in the management and public accountability of large sections of the civil service as a result of Next Steps, there is still a long way to go. Specific changes which we would recommend include:

- the methods of defining ministerial and agency responsibilities has to be revisited and clarified. This may include having quite different relationships for different agency types;

- consideration should be given, as part of the Prior Options process, to a much more radical look at designing organisations to fit the functions to be performed, regardless of existing departmental boundaries;

- in some small agencies with low political salience there may be a case for reverting to having a departmental senior manager act as 'owner' rather than a minister;

- some agencies may be transferred to non-departmental public bodies (NDPB) or even public corporation status (within a specific legal framework) to distance them more clearly from direct ministerial control and responsibility;

- for those agencies which remain reporting directly to ministers, there is a need to get a much clearer responsibility definition established than presently seems to be accepted, especially by ministers;

- single, annual, quasi-contract covering: responsibilities, rights, resources (including three-year projections) and targets (including three-year projections) – replacing framework documents, business, corporate and efficiency plans.

- KPIs: a balanced system is needed linking PIs to objectives and covering inputs, outputs and efficiency indicators;

- annual reports with more information in the text about use of resources against objectives, efficiency and effectiveness information;
- reconsideration of the use of resource accounts only.

Note

Readers wishing to get a more detailed description of the executive agency experience are referred to: Colin Talbot, *Ministers and Agencies – Control, Performance and Accountability*, London, Chartered Institute of Public Finance and Accountancy (CIPFA), 1996. This paper is derived in part from that report.

References

Carter, N., Klein, R. and Day, P. (1992), *How Organisations Measure Success – The Use of Performance Indicators in Government*, Routledge

Civil Service Statistics (1995), London, HMSO

Customs and Excise (1995), *Management Plan*, 1995-96 to 1997-98, Customs and Excise, London

Efficiency Unit (May 1995), *Resource Management Systems*, London, HMSO

Efficiency and Effectiveness Group (November 1995), *Guidance for Development and Use of Efficiency Plans*, London, HMSO

Flynn, N. (1994), *Change in the Civil Service*, CIPFA

Helco, H. and Wildavsky, A. (1974), *The Private Government of Public Money*, Macmillan, London

Hood, C. (1991), 'A Public Management for All Seasons?' *Public Administration*, Vol. 69, No. 1, Blackwell

Kemp, Sir Peter (1989), 'Managing Performance in Central Government', in Beeton, D. and Terry, F. (eds), *Evaluating Public Service Performance* (1989), Public Finance Foundation, CIPFA

Jenkins, K. et al (1988), *Improving Management in Government: The Next Steps*, London, HMSO

Learmont (1995), *Review of Prison Service Security in England and Wales and The Escape from Parkhurst Prison on Tuesday 3 January 1995 – The Learmont Report,* Cm 3020, London, HMSO

Office of Public Service (1994), *Next Steps Review 1994*, London, HMSO

Office of Public Service (1995), *Guidance on Agency Reviews*, Cabinet Office (OPS) December

Office of Public Service (1996), *Next Steps Review 1995*, London, HMSO

Ouchi, W. (1981), *Theory Z*, Addison Wesley. For further exploration of these ideas see also Thompson, G., Frances, J., Levacic, R. and Mitchell, J. (1991), *Markets, Hierarchies and Networks*, London, Sage Publications

Pollit, C. (1991), *Managerialism and the Public Services: the Anglo-American Experience,* Oxford, Blackwell.

The Implications for Top Management of Managing Strategic Issues

A Response to Colin Talbot
Paddy Teahon

Professor Talbot's paper is particularly thoughtful and, in the light of the stage we have reached in Ireland in implementing the Strategic Management Initiative and *Delivering Better Government*, (the report prepared for the government by the Co-Ordinating Group of Secretaries), most relevant. I would like to offer some comments in two areas:

- how should government, the civil and the public service be managed: what is the best or preferred approach?

- what are the implications for the Irish situation of what Professor Talbot has said about the management of public agencies in the UK?

I believe it is important for top management to be particularly clear about the context of strategic management. This begs the question: how should we approach strategic management in a public service context? In my view there are a number of possible models relevant to the management of government. These have been particularly well summarised by Henry Mintzberg in a recent article 'Managing Government, Governing Management' (1996) and with due attribution to him I have set out those models in Figure 1. These are:

- Government as Machine, where the key is control;
- Virtual Government, where the key is privatisation and contracting out;
- Performance Control, where the key is measurement and which links with the first model of Government as Machine;
- Normative Control, where the key is to select, socialise and judge; and finally
- Government as Network, where the key is to connect, communicate and collaborate.

In my view the approach to the management of government inherent in what Professor Talbot spoke about centres on models 1-3. I believe that we need to take the useful aspects of the performance approach, but that critically we need to combine those with model 4, the Normative approach, and 5, the Network approach, in the Irish situation. These latter models are well attuned to what is best in public service and have a clear focus on the delivery of excellent services and can thereby overcome the potentially negative effort of bureaucracy.

The normative approach places particular importance on:

- values and attitudes;
- people in the public service who are dedicated to an integrated social system;
- accepted principles in place of imposed plans;
- vision as a guiding umbrella instead of targets as a directing force, subject, of course, to budgetary controls;
- relationships and leadership based on trust;

Figure 1:

Model 1: Government as Machine

Control, control, control

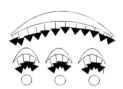

Model 2: Virtual Government

Privatise, contract, negotiate

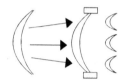

Model 3: Performance Control

Isolate, assign, measure

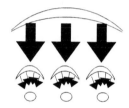

Model 4: Normative Control

Select, socialise, judge

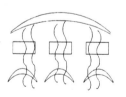

Model 5: Government as Network

Connect, communicate, collaborate

- judgement and assessment of performance by the wise consideration of experienced people, including recipients of the service.

In my view the normative model can link closely with Government as Network, particularly so in the case of a small country like Ireland. The network approach places particular importance on the value of cooperation at a variety of levels rather than a competitive or imposed approach.

I will turn now to my second area of comment, namely the relevance of the British experience to what we are now embarking on in Ireland in implementing SMI and *Delivering Better Government*. For me the core of Professor Talbot's thoughtful presentation is the figure dividing the work of government departments in four, namely policy, governance, management and support services. If I interpret Professor Talbot correctly on this and its working through in the UK public service change process, he would say we need to be particularly concerned with:

- resources;
- a simple approach;
- avoiding the 'Whitehall Village' syndrome; and
- good communication.

I believe the approach we are now adopting in Ireland of having strategy statements, translating these into action programmes to implement strategy and having a monitoring system to report on progress is, in that sense, the right model.

Professor Talbot's paper should forewarn us of traps, in particular I believe if the centre of the civil service attempts to exercise undue control and if the link to clear ministerial accountability in parliament is broken. In my judgement we need to opt for clarity in producing strategy statements, clear and succinct translation of these into action programmes, and a clear-headed system to monitor progress. We should do this within an approach which: values performance; gives full weight in a normative way to what is best about public service; and which recognises the significant advantages of a cooperative approach through networking, a factor which is particularly relevant and feasible in a country the size of Ireland.

Reference

Mintzberg, H. (1996), 'Managing Government, Governing Management', *Harvard Business Review*, vol. 74, no. 3, May/June

Acting on Strategic Change

Donal de Buitleir

Introduction

When I accepted the invitation to present this paper, it was with some reluctance, not least in case in might be thought that here was yet another case of someone in the private sector (albeit for a relatively short time) telling the public sector how to organise affairs. That is not my intention. What I want to do is to put forward some thoughts based on my experience in four different areas; the reader can decide how relevant this may be to the current challenges facing the public sector.

Early in my career, I felt that stability was the norm, even if this were punctuated by periods of significant change. This has altered. Change now is not something that we have to go through on occasions, and when completed we can get back to something we call normality. In the modern world change is the norm and it has been aptly said 'Standing still is the fastest way of moving backwards in a rapidly changing world'.

I see no reason to change the view I expressed almost five years ago that management and change is more difficult in the public sector than in the private sector (de Buitleir 1991).

I am very grateful to Catherine Burke, Dr. Liam Gorman, Mary Grogan, Liam Hennessy and Professor Patrick Lynch for their help in preparing this paper. Views expressed should not be attributed to them. All errors and opinions are my responsibility.

In the private sector the objectives are generally very clear and measurable. In the public sector objectives tend to be less clear and may be in conflict. Important social and political objectives may not always sit easily with the need for efficiency and effectiveness.

A further disadvantage from which the public service suffers is a lack of competition. Innovation is difficult but essential (Porter 1990, p 119). Often it is the spur of competition which facilitates innovation. If you have a choice – to change or go out of business – change appears attractive. Competition also allows opposition to be overcome. The non-market environment of much of the public sector does not provide an environment which makes change easy.

Strategic

The word strategic is overused and I am not certain that it means the same thing to everyone. According to Jim O'Donnell's invaluable *Word Gloss* (1990) strategy, coming from the Greek word 'strategos', is defined as 'the series of steps needed to win a campaign or other major objective'.

In my view, change must have three dimensions to be termed strategic; it should be important, it should have medium to long-term implications and it should be irreversible (at least, within a reasonable time frame).

Committees

Before dealing with the important issue of organisational change, I want to talk a little bit about the use of committees consisting wholly or partly of members drawn from outside the civil service. A major mechanism for achieving strategic change in the public sector is the establishment of the committee or commission of inquiry. I have been involved with seven of these bodies in the last fifteen years as either secretary, member or chairman. These bodies have been at local, national and European level. I believe that such committees can be made significantly more successful if they are structured in a particular way.

In general, the success of these bodies in achieving strategic change has been limited and in my view more limited than the quality of the analysis would have justified. When I ask myself why this is so, I have come to the conclusion that at least part of the reason is the way the committees have been structured.

A committee or commission of inquiry is established usually only when the normal means of determining policy are unable to deal with the problem. Like major operations, they are tried only on patients who are already very ill. In fact, the establishment of a commission could be seen as an indicator of failure of the department in whose policy area the commission is established. The usual structure is that a group of private sector individuals or representatives of various interests is given terms of reference. Supported by a secretariat usually drawn from the civil service, the commission is charged with the task of producing a public report outlining what should be done. Even allowing for the fact that the tasks allocated to commissions are difficult and often are political 'hot potatoes', their record of success in terms of getting their recommendations implemented are disappointing.

I want to raise some questions about the process of how we attempted tax reform in Ireland. The model used for the *Commission on Taxation* was a well-known one: an independent commission of eminent persons and experts was set up to examine the issues and make recommendations. The danger with this model is that if the commission's analysis produces a radical blueprint the political/administrative system may not be able to absorb it. Politicians, officials and others who will not have participated in the debates inside the commission may be unable, at least initially, to digest and cope with a set of radical proposals. The danger is compounded by the fact that commissions are only set up when conventional methods of solving problems have failed; the issues that they are usually given to examine require radical solutions.

My thinking on this issue has been influenced significantly by my experience on the Ruding Committee. This committee was a group of eight independent experts (some of whom were accompanied by advisers) established by the EU Commission to advise on corporation tax harmonisation (a very difficult and complex subject). The committee deliberated for fifteen months and reported on 18 March, 1992.

The interesting feature of this committee was that Commission officials, up to and including the Director-General of the Taxation Directorate, attended all the meetings and participated in the debate. This had two effects; first the EU Commission was privy to the thinking of the committee and was able to bring points to the attention of the committee before matters were decided. Secondly, the Commission officials were themselves influenced by the debates in the committee and were fully up to speed on the matter. Thirdly, the fact that the Commission officials did not have to sign the report made it easier to propose more radical options. The results were dramatic. Less than three months after the Ruding Committee reported, the Commission published its reaction to the report and what it proposed to do about it.

The contrast with the Commission on Taxation could not be more striking. The debates in that commission were characterised by an openness and an intellectual honesty that I have rarely found. All who had the privilege to participate in the exercise learned a great deal and changed their views significantly. Unfortunately, civil servants and politicians did not have this opportunity. As a result they found it very difficult to understand and cope with the radical nature of the commission's proposals.

Consider the fate of the Commission on Taxation if, say, the Secretary of the Department of Finance had participated in its meetings. I believe it would have been very different; in fact, it is very likely that both the recommendations of the commission and the response of the government would have been different. My conclusion, based on my experience of operating under both the Irish and EU systems, is that in future the leading policy makers in a department in whose area of responsibility an independent commission is established should attend all meetings with a right to participate fully. However, the civil servants should not be members of the commission. Government should be committed in advance to publishing a response to the commission's proposals within a specified time limit, which would set out its decisions and the reasons for them.

Some may argue that the very slow progress in relation to the implementation of the Ruding Report disproves my analysis. However, in my view this is more related to the fact that decisions in the fiscal area at EU level require unanimity rather than to the failure of the model I am suggesting.

The structure I am proposing was used in the Advisory Committee on Third-Level Student Support Schemes, which I chaired (Stationery Office 1993) and worked extremely well. Admittedly in a relatively less complex area, the report was produced in seven months and a departmental response was issued three months later. This very quick response was due entirely to the fact that key officials in the Department of Education were fully involved in discussing all the recommendations, had a sense of ownership of them and had a knowledge of what was involved which could not be gained merely from a dispassionate reading of a report which happens to land on one's desk. Indeed, many of the important insights in that report came from the civil servants who attended the meetings.

I have had experience of working on committees preparing reports for publication of which civil servants have been members. In general, I think this is not a good structure from both the point of view of the committee and the individual civil servants and their departments. This is not to deny that the expertise of civil servants is not valuable; indeed it is essential. However, I believe that it is easier to get more options into the public domain if civil servants do not have to show their hands early and can 'keep their powder dry' until the relevant memorandum for the government is being prepared. It is , of course, essential that civil servants are prepared to attend meetings of committees of which they are not formal members; otherwise the benefits of the structure I am proposing would be lost.

In highly complex and controversial areas it might be useful to establish a public forum to debate the findings of a commission. The National Educational Convention provides a useful model in this area. Such fora may provide valuable means of getting acceptance of the constraints that surround any complex policy area and of building a consensus about what needs to be done from a menu of realistic policy options.

Organisational Change

In my experience the success or failure of the organisations I have worked in to date have been highly correlated with the quality of leadership provided by the top management in the organisation. The chief executive is particularly important in getting change, but failing that a significant individual or group in the leadership may fill the vacuum.

One may distinguish between transformational and transactional leadership. Where transactional managers make only minor adjustments in the organisation's mission, structure and human resource management, transformational leaders not only make major changes in these three areas but they also evoke fundamental changes in the basic political and cultural systems of the organisation.

Dynamics of Change

Organisations do not change unless there is a trigger (often from outside) which indicates that change is needed. It is, I believe, much better if the internal management of the organisation sees the need for change. If they do, it is likely to be embarked on earlier and more successfully than if it has to be imposed from outside. Organisational failure often goes much too far before enough external pressure builds up to force change on a reluctant management.

Once the need for change has been accepted there are three identifiable programmes of activity associated with transformational leadership. These are:

• the creation of a vision

• the mobilisation of commitment

• the institutionalisation of change.

I now want to look at a number of case studies to illustrate the importance of the various steps in the process of change.

Self - Assessment : A Case Study

'Recent years have seen far-reaching changes in the tax administration system' is something of an understatement taken from the 1989 Annual Report of the Revenue Commissioners (page 3). In my view, the transformation of the Office of the Revenue Commissioners over the past ten years provides a dramatic example of what can be achieved even in unpromising circumstances.

Dissatisfaction with the performance of tax collection had been building up over a period of some years. In the main, the pressure for change was externally generated and became irresistible. Some may not remember the position in the mid-1980s. According to the Commission on Taxation (Fifth Report, October 1985),

> The administration of taxation in Ireland has virtually broken down. Non-compliance is a major problem. The situation will get worse unless the evident problems are tackled quickly and with determination. Radical measures are needed.

The Fifth Report of the Commission on Taxation was an important catalyst for change here and led to the appointment of an International Monetary Fund (IMF) study team to examine the question of self-assessment. The fact that the main author of the commission's report (not the present writer), who was a convinced advocate of self-assessment, acted as the secretary to the IMF team greatly assisted that examination.

In the Revenue in the mid-1980s, it was the pressure from government unable to withstand the public controversy generated by the publication of large amounts of tax outstanding that led to change. For example, the Report of the Comptroller and Auditor General showed total tax arrears of £1,318 million for the self-employed sector as at 31 May,1988. This figure was roughly five times the expected annual tax yield from this sector. Insiders knew that these arrears, based largely on estimated assessments, were largely illusory and did not represent a 'pot of gold' which could be used to reduce the burden of tax on the PAYE sector if only the Revenue would get their act together. As two people directly involved in tax administration at the time have written:

The annual publication of this large arrears figure created a strong sense of grievance in the minds of other taxpayers and gave rise to unfounded beliefs that the serious imbalances in the Irish public finances could be greatly ameliorated if this figure could only be collected. More seriously for the administration of the tax system, this largely notional figure had a tendency to gum up the works of collection of the real arrears; and the attempts by the tax authorities to explain the figure away, however accurate and laudable, tended to reflect badly on the credibility of the Finance and Revenue authorities. (Cassells and Thornhill in Sandford 1993).

Public confidence in what Patrick Lynch called 'the quality of the official mind' was lost at least as far as tax administration was concerned.

The need for change unleashes mixed forces, in particular a strong negative individual and organisational resistance. These may include cultural factors. For example, in the Revenue experience, I believe that there was a feeling that self-assessment would downgrade technical tax expertise which was highly valued in the culture of the organisation. There was also a fear of what tax audits on the premises of taxpayers might entail for staff who previously raised queries in writing from behind a desk.

Change, certainly radical change, requires transformational leadership. In the case of the Revenue this leadership was provided primarily by the late Frank Cassells.

The importance of a changed vision in the case of the Revenue is stressed by Cassells and Thornhill

... most important of all was the emerging awareness in the political and official mind that large scale tax compliance cannot be achieved solely by threats and penalties. There also arose an awareness that a tax system, of itself, if badly structured, could contribute to poor

From Intent to Action

tax compliance simply by its own inefficiencies, whether perceived or real (p.154).

The vision or focus of the Revenue was changed from 'persecuting compliant taxpayers' which is what was happening. If a self-employed person sent in his accounts he was likely to get two pages of queries back on them while, if he did nothing, very little happened and then only after a long time. The changed vision was one of encouraging voluntary compliance and tackling non-compliance in a serious way.

A number of initiatives were taken to mobilise commitment to change inside the organisation (Cassells and Hennessy 1989). These included:

*   the establishment of a planning group of senior management to oversee and initiate developments;

*   the holding of regular residential conferences for middle management to improve communications and obtain feed-back on development initiatives;

*   the establishment of training courses to promote greater awareness among staff of the needs of the public as 'customers' and to provide them with new skills to deal with the public. The customer focus was reinforced by a comprehensive Taxpayers' Charter which was given extensive coverage in the media and displayed prominently in tax offices.

Institutional changes were announced in the 1988 budget speech and enacted into law. The legal basis of the old system was effectively dismantled thereby making the change irreversible.

The great success of the Revenue is recognised widely. However, in successful organisations the greatest danger can be the feeling that the job of change has been completed and that what is now required is consolidation. Much has been achieved, but the job of organisational change never ends and much remains to be done to meet the challenges offered by developments in technology and the quest for greater efficiency in a highly competitive world. Arguably the success of the organisation makes further change more difficult because the external pressure for change is reduced. The challenge for the current generation of leaders of the organisation is to generate the vision and commitment to ensure that the organisation fulfills its potential to be among the leading Revenue organisations in the world. To set that vision and measure its success by the achievement of published benchmarks is perhaps the next task facing the organisation.

Public Service Reform in the Mid-1980s

John Boland's attempt to transform the public service in the mid-1980s underlines the importance of institutionalising change so that it will persist after the personalities driving it have moved on.

Creation of a vision

Boland published a government white paper *Serving the Country Better* (1985) in which he attempted to create a vision of the future. This vision was however directed primarily at taxpayers and voters who had relatively little interest in the process of public service reform. He had little to say to the staff who were extremely concerned with the issues. Little attempt was made to explain the proposals to the people who were most directly affected.

Mobilisation of commitment

This was perhaps the weakest part of the reform proposals. Boland, some might argue quite justifiably, made a number of speeches which were perceived as attacking the public service for its outdated practices and inefficiencies. These were received very negatively by key groups of staff which interpreted his attitude as an attack on themselves As a result it engendered deep hostility towards Boland and his proposals.

One could not imagine a less successful way of attempting to mobilise commitment to change.

Institutionalisation of change

Boland's greatest success was, I believe, in the area of institutionalising change. He ensured that in future all appointments at assistant secretary and secretary level in departments would be on merit, rather than seniority subject to fitness as had been the usual practice. This radically changed the systems of selection, appraisal and reward. In future it became important to have a record of achievement in one's area of work if one were to argue for future promotion, rather than just to be able to show that you kept the minister out of trouble.

Boland was fortunate in introducing the new changes just before a large wave of retirements took place in the higher civil service. This meant that a critical mass of individuals appointed under the new system were in place within a relatively short period. In my view, the transformation brought about by the Top Level Appointments Committee (TLAC) system has been of great significance and will endure long after most people will ever have heard of John Boland, thus underlining the particular importance of putting in place institutional mechanisms which carry on the change. Indeed the TLAC reforms were important in helping to progress the reforms in the Revenue Commissioners which I discussed earlier. Of a top management group of eighteen noted in the 1990 Annual Report, only two had not been appointed under the new procedures.

AIB 2000

These attempts at reform were to a large degree imposed on the organisations from outside, at least initially. In my view it is better if the organisation itself sees the need for change and acts on it. This applies from two perspectives. It reduces resistance and the change process can start earlier.

I would like to briefly outline the current change management programme in Allied Irish Banks (AIB) Group. This may be of interest for two reasons; firstly, it has elements of the three things which I believe support the change process; vision, an attempt to mobilise commitment and certain institutional features; and secondly it involves a major focus on the customer which is also an important theme of the Strategic Management Initiative.

Some years ago we came to the view in AIB that despite our current success, a number of developments on the horizon implied that we could no longer assume that success would continue without adapting to the changes driven by increased competition, developments in technology and entry to EMU. Group management of an organisation that is relatively successful has perceived the need for change, which can now take place at the right time and at the right pace.

The diagnosis we made was straightforward and easily understood by all our people. We could no longer assume AIB would continue to hold its current volume of business and profitability. So, in 1994 we started a search for a new vision, one that would take us up to the end of the century. We considered four options:

- continue as before
- launch a dramatic cost-cutting programme
- impose a 'top/down' management change programme
- attempt to involve staff throughout the organisation in a vision-led change experience.

We chose the latter option – involve staff throughout the organisation in a vision-led change experience.

We thought this strategy had the best chance of encouraging ownership of business issues at all levels. It would encourage fresh thinking and new ideas from people across the organisation. In short, we felt it would deliver the right changes for AIB at the right pace – and if not we would revisit our options again.

This approach put the focus on what we needed to do differently to thrive in the future.

We started with a vision. This was to make AIB 'wherever we operate, the leading Irish banking group, creating superior value for our customers and shareholders'. We would measure our success in four ways:

- the level of customer satisfaction
- the return to our shareholders
- the contributions of individuals and teams
- our performance as a good corporate citizen.

We also developed a set of values that would guide our attitudes and actions, such as customer focus, high performance with integrity and professionalism.

After extensive consultation, what we call AIB 2000 was launched in Autumn 1994. In the UK and Ireland, more than 11,000 AIB personnel (from the chief executive to the porters) attended 820 day-long sessions, in groups of fifteen or less, in just three months – the biggest communications exercise ever undertaken in AIB.

Institutional changes

A most important element in the change programme was the imperative of improving the level of customer service. This is the only protection in an era of increased competition. There are two institutional changes which I believe have focused attention on improving customer service. Remember 'customer service is remembered long after price is forgotten'.

The first is our Customer Service Awards programme which came into operation in 1995. Under this scheme awards were introduced for both individual (quarterly) and team (annual) performance in the area of customer service. Individuals are nominated for awards by other staff members. Nominations are put through an evaluation process which obtains line manager input and decision by an evaluation committee. The evaluation committees are chaired by a senior executive and consist of a cross-section of staff within the Group. For each quarter, twenty winners from all parts of the organisation are chosen. The individual award is worth £500 on which the bank pays the tax.

The team awards are made on the basis of submissions by individual teams who comprise between two and thirty people. These submissions are then examined by evaluation committees in different parts of the Group. The results of surveys of customer service are also available for consideration in making the evaluations. As a result a number of teams are chosen to make presentations. The final evaluation committee is chaired by the chief executive and the top eleven teams are invited to make presentations. Members of the overall winning team receive an award of £1,000 each and the ten runners up receive £200 each. Again, the bank pays the tax.

Award schemes of this nature are only one element in the drive to meet organisational goals. Reward and recognition schemes are generally focused around exceeding defined expectations within a specific time period. For the process to impact fully on behaviour in the organisation, the customer service requirements of work units need to be followed up at performance reviews, interviews, promotions and business reviews. One example of this was the development of a customer service best practice code from the information contained in customer service award nominations.

The second institutional mechanism for achieving change that I want to discuss is the AIB Customer Service Measurement Programme. This is important because 'what gets measured gets done'. The measurement of service quality in AIB has three elements:

- the first is a national survey of the banking population based on intereviews to determine customer expectations of a number of key service issues;

- the second is a survey of each of 300 branches in Ireland using personal interviews of customers as they leave the branch. Its main purpose is to measure how customers rate branch service on the key service issues identified in the national survey;

- the third element uses professional researchers to measure service levels experienced and impressions during telephone and branch visits to each of 300 branches.

The results of all these surveys are fed back to local management and form an element in the annual review of performance of individual managers. The annual review of performance also has an important influence on remuneration. This ensures that service quality issues get management attention.

It is too early to gauge fully the effect of these schemes on improving customer service; this will only be clear when we have data tracking this over a period of years. The initial indications are positive. However, that is beside the main point I want to make which is that institutional mechanisms that go beyond personalities are essential in achieving sustainable strategic change.

Conclusion

What does all this signify for the prospects of achieving change in the civil service ?

While most outside observers wish the process of change well, there have been enough false dawns in the past to make one wary about making predictions.

The vision of a high performance civil service 'competitive by reference to international comparisons and benchmarks' is clearly there and is very welcome. It seems to me that there is a leadership group in the civil service that sees the need for change and is committed to it. A major task is to mobilise commitment to achieving the vision at all levels of the civil service and to have institutional mechanisms to ensure that progress towards the vision is measured and that its achievement makes an important difference to the individuals charged with the task.

References

de Buitleir, Donal (1991), 'Reflections on Management in the Public Service', *Seirbhis Phoiblí*, Vol. 12.1, Nollag

Cassells, Frank and Hennessy, Liam (1989), 'Long Run Policy Planning as a Means of Improving Tax Compliance – The Irish Perspective', Presentation to OECD, October

Cassells, Frank and Thornhill, Don (1993), 'Self Assessment and Administrative Tax Reform in Ireland', in *Key Issues in Tax Reform*, Cedric Sandford (ed), Chapter 7, Bath, Fiscal Publications

Commission on Taxation (1985), 'Tax Administration', Fifth Report, October

O'Donnell, Jim (1990), *Word Gloss*, Dublin, Institute of Public Administration

Porter, Michael E. (1990), *The Competitive Advantage of Nations*

Report on the National Education Convention by the Convention Secretariat (1994), Editor John Coolahan, Government Publications

Report of the Advisory Committee on Third-Level Student Support (1993), Dublin, Stationery Office

Tichy, Noel M. and Ulrich, David O. (1984), 'The Leadership Challenge – A Call for the Transformational Leader', *Sloan Management Review*

White Paper, *Serving the Country Better* (1985), Dublin, Stationery Office

Acting on Strategic Change in Organisations

A Response to Donal de Buitleir
John Fitzgerald

Donal de Buitleir's opening remarks are statements of fact that, nonetheless, need to be stated and restated, principally:

1. The management of change is more difficult in the public service. This is obviously so as the pressures are different, the structure of rewards is different, there are political sensitivities which must be observed and so on.

2. Private sector objectives are more clear and more measurable. Again, this is correct. The profit motive is the engine which drives most of what happens in the private sector; profit or lack of profit, is easily measured. Measures of performance in the public sector are not easily identified, and even when they are identified there are, for example, quality issues which are not determined by market forces.

3. There is the absence of competition in the public service i.e. you do not go out of business if you do not change.

4. Strategy is not so easily defined. Again, particularly true in the public sector; where do you draw the line between strategy and operational issues?

There are other barriers to progress in the public sector which go beyond these points. For instance, rewards are very much the same for those who perform and for those who do not. It is not easy to generate debate on long term policy in a system which is motivated by the need to respond to representational matters at national and local level.

Given all these issues it is to the credit of the public service that major structural change has been implemented as effectively as it has been. Donal de Buitleir, in his paper, instances the experience of the Revenue Commissioners who have improved their performance to the extent that they now extract money while making the tax payer feel good about it. There are other examples.

I have myself had direct involvement in the most fundamental restructuring of local government in the history of the state. Local government in Dublin, representing about one-third of local government in the country, has been transformed by the creation of three new counties around the city. The capacity of the public sector staff who did this has been much admired. The result is a form of local government which is much more relevant to the public, and which is acknowledged to be successful.

The decision to go this road emanated from a succession of white papers and the deliberations of successive governments over a long period of time. However, once the final decision was made in 1991, it was implemented with remarkable speed. This was so largely because the positions of those who were to implement that decision – county managers designate – were created as part of the legislative framework which surrounded it. Hence, a core group of people existed who had an interest in speedy implementation. This approach was

The concept of strategic management is now all-pervasive and is certainly driving changes in attitudes and is most welcome.

Bureaucratic structures set up to serve the requirements of the last century have no place in the modern environment which requires speedy reaction, fast decision making and an acceptance that, even if the users of a service do not pay directly, they are entitled to exactly the same response as if they did.

There is also acceptance that the concept of devolution must push responsibility, and the authority that goes with that responsibility, down through the structure so that decisions are made at the level at which they can be best made. There is no longer any acceptance of a system which requires that relatively trivial decisions must be referred upwards to ministerial level, or county manager level in local government.

What is in it for public sector employees? Not much by way of financial rewards certainly, though there is scope for 'awards' schemes as outlined in the paper.

However, most public service staff look for little more than the freedom to get on with what they do best and the satisfaction and pride associated with doing a good job in an organisation which they can be proud to be part of. That is nothing less than their entitlement.

However, there is always the concept of public accountability which, inevitably, accompanies the knowledge that we are responsible for the control and disbursement of public funds. This concept of public accountability does not encourage risk taking in the public service. Implementation of structural change inevitably involves risk taking. If this is to be encouraged – and we all agree that it should be encouraged – the political system must accept that risk taking is inevitably accompanied by some failures and the political system must be prepared to accommodate and tolerate this.

Finally, as Donal de Buitleir points out in his paper, the need for change should not imply failure. The most successful companies are those that recognise the need for ongoing review and change in such a way that success can lead to even greater success.

Rapporteur's Report

Frank Litton

My task here is a difficult one. The papers of the conference are so rich in concepts, that any quick attempt to provide a coherent summary is difficult to achieve. The difficulty of my task is evidence enough that the proceedings of the conference have done justice to the complexity of implementing strategic management in the public sector.

Perhaps it is worth reflecting on that complexity and its characteristics. As I listened to the conference discussions I was reminded of an observation of the Canadian political philosopher Charles Taylor. He reports that two metaphors dominate our understanding of the role of knowledge in our lives. We speak of knowledge as a 'tool': it produces those understandings of how the world works that allow us shape and manipulate it to serve our interests. This metaphor tells us knowledge is at its most powerful when it provides us with well-grounded techniques. The move to understanding knowledge in this way underpinned the scientific revolution, and the success of that revolution validates it.

Our tradition also allows us speak of knowledge as 'vision'. To come to know something is to come to see it as it really is. This can be supremely difficult. I am reminded of the artist who when asked if he painted what he saw, replied: no, I paint in order to discover what I see. I suppose we find the most powerful expression of this understanding of knowledge as vision in Plato. Charles Taylor draws this distinction between two ways of understanding knowledge not to find one superior to the other. Both clearly capture important aspects of reality. He points out that the predominance which the metaphor of 'knowledge as tool' has enjoyed in the modern era is increasingly challenged, as philosophers and others argue that 'knowledge as vision' provides a better guide to how we might understand the many problems that beset us in political, social and organisational life.

Anyhow, as I listened to the conference deliberations it occurred to me that the metaphor of 'knowledge as vision' was the appropriate metaphor for the kind of knowledge that is central to strategic management. Brendan Tuohy spoke in his paper of the 'overt' and 'covert' organisations. He suggested, I think, that what we take to be the realities of and for our organisations are often little more than the projections of the feelings or prejudgements of the 'covert' organisation. It takes a real effort to move beyond these shadowy reflections, to leave Plato's cave as it were, and to see things as they really are. This effort is at the heart of strategic management. The effort to bring others to see things in the same way is at the heart of implementing strategy. Brendan Tuohy struck another platonic theme when he argued the importance of constant questioning. Drawing people into dialogue where 'group think' is challenged and the status quo questioned, is he tells us, an integral part of the strategic management process. Many others things were said to-day which pointed to the same conclusion: strategic management is not usefully seen as a 'technique'. Professor Bryson provided a most interesting discussion of forward mapping and backward mapping as two contrasting but complementary parts of implementation planning. Forward mapping moves from the understanding of the enterprise as a whole to encompass each particular operation as its expression. Backward mapping moves us in the opposite direction; the particular operation and its requirement brings us back to the whole that is necessary to sustain it. We could say each provides a necessary 'horizon' in which to view the organisation, and that the two 'horizons' need to be merged if we are to see things in the round. There is no one absolute point of view from which everything is revealed. Rather we need dialogue in which different perspectives can blend.

Professor Bryson emphasised the importance of leadership in the implementation of strategy. In his preferred definition 'public leadership is the inspiration and mobilisation of others to undertake collective action in pursuit of the common good'. At the most general level this entails the representation of this common good and the identification of feasible actions towards it. In the details of implementation it involves informing the perspectives of the various actors with the strategic orientation; whether they be engaged in budgetary politics or operational planning.

Metaphors can mislead. I think I would misrepresent much of what we have heard to-day if I reported that 'knowledge as technique' had no place in implementing strategic management. Professor Bryson demonstrated the merit of various techniques. In particular his nuanced account of the five types of strategic planning demonstrates the value of looking for appropriate 'tools' to implement strategy. Nonetheless, he also points to the danger that attaches to these techniques. In his paper he tells us the systems often become too number-oriented; captured by forecasts that are inappropriate and conservative. Perhaps it can be put this way: there are indeed techniques that can help us find and aim at the target. But they themselves are not the target, and faithfully implementing them should not be confused with moving towards it.

No one listening to to-day's discussion could be in any doubt that implementing strategic management in the public sector involves changing points of view. Those concerned must come to a new understanding of their organisations and their place within them. As students of organisation culture continually remind us, an individual's point of view is rooted in the evaluations he makes. Where we stand is given by what we stand for. Consequently, the required cultural change will involve changes in our ideas of the goods we should expect to find and serve in the public sector. We should be prepared to make explicit our political philosophy so that it may be criticised, developed and deepened.

Donal De Buitléir's illuminating case studies exemplify the importance of leadership and cultural transformation. But he also points to the valuable lesson that cultural change on its own is not sufficient. The new orientations must be translated into changed practices and control systems. Ideas that do not find appropriate institutional expression do not survive. The most inspired vision, expressed in the most cogent and comprehensive strategy, will achieve nothing unless there are structures in place that can coordinate the efforts to realise it.

The deliberations of this conference have raised many issues that should be addressed in the process of developing new understanding, forming new evaluations and seeking institutional forms suitable to them. I would like to highlight three of the most important brought to our attention.

Professor Talbot's paper raised important questions for us in Ireland. The case for executive agencies is a beguiling one. It promises something for everyone; for the taxpayer a more efficient, effective, performance-orientated public service; for the citizen with new right anxieties, tighter control over budget-maximising bureaucrats; for the public service manager a space in which to develop their management skills in devising and implementing operations. Devlin recommended we move the Irish civil service in this direction nearly thirty years ago. Lectures in public administration invoke the 'lack of political will' to explain why the recommendation was not acted upon. There was no lack of 'political will' across the water yet, as Professor Talbot told us, progress has been patchy. Some of the difficulties that have inhibited progress are difficulties that attend any attempt at organisational change. In particular, cultural change is difficult. It cannot be commanded. It takes time. Old points of view persist and weaken the motivation to make the changes succeed. Professor Talbot's researches show that the revaluation which would accord status and worth to the successful management of operations as distinct from policy work has yet to happen. These difficulties are compounded by flaws in the case for executive agencies. That case overlooked important complexities in the management of public business. Professor Talbot points to the heart of the matter when he reminds us of the traditional 'policy-administration' paradox. This is the fact that policy and administration are separable in concept but not in practice. The wholly desirable objective underlying the move to executive agencies is to give a new importance to managing programmes and services. We should maintain that objective, while realising it cannot be achieved without due attention to the special problems of corporate governance, and policy formation characteristic of the civil service.

Another important issue arises when we accept the symbiotic relationship between structure and strategy. Strategy defines the business an organisation is in, while structure orchestrates the division of labour necessary to deliver what that business demands. Any significant changes in that business will require consequent changes in structure. As government departments develop strategies, they are likely to discover serious mismatches between what the new strategy demands and what the old structure can deliver. The implementation of the strategic management initiative is, then, likely to require changes in the structures of departments. The problem is that the changes needed will differ from department to department. Some departments may find it necessary to move to more elaborate, finely tuned bureaucracies, while others will discover their strategy entails a move away from bureaucracy.

The implications are clear. Uniform structures across departments, the traditional way of sustaining the unity of the civil service, will no longer be tenable. New methods for maintaining the unity must be found. These will be capable of supporting the diversity of structural forms demanded by the complexities of ever-changing environments. I suppose this particular problem poses special challenges for the central departments.

The third issue concerns the impact of the strategic management initiative on the relationships between the political and administrative systems. Can the strategic management initiative succeed without some reordering of that relationship? Perhaps we need to rethink that relationship.

The business of the administrative system is to provide the state with a strong executive capacity that can formulate and implement policy. The business of the political system is to give citizens and elected representatives an authoritative voice in the deliberations that shape public policy. The two businesses are, of course, closely related. Without an executive capacity the deliberations of public representatives would be of little consequence. If the public representatives lacked final authority, the executive powers of the state would pass into the hands of an elite, distant from, unconcerned with, and possibly hostile to the needs of the citizens. Should both fail, we would have neither executive capacity nor public accountability.

Recent times have seen moves to strengthen both systems. Legislation is being formulated to make government more transparent and to strengthen the power of Oireachtas committees. Today we have been discussing important initiatives to enhance the policy-formulating capacities of the civil service. We need, I suppose, to consider how these 'twin tracks' can be united in an improved design for democracy.

One concluding point: it is clear that strategic management will not be successfully implemented without cultural changes followed by structural reforms. In this context Donal De Buitléir's well-informed account of why some commissions of enquiry lead to change while others do not showed that involvement in discussions proves an indispensable education. We learn in the process, not from its conclusions. It is in the play of conversation that horizons merge, new points of view are found and acceptable solutions discovered. I suppose we should think seriously about how fora for these discussions can best be established. As Brendan Tuohy has argued, they are needed within departments. They are also needed across departments. It is the whole administrative system that is to be transformed and there are issues that bear on its underlying unity that require a system-wide perspective.